Swallow's Nest

A Feminine Reading of the Psalms

Marchiene Vroon Rienstra

William B. Eerdmans Publishing Company ❧ Grand Rapids, Michigan

Friendship Press ❧ New York

Gracewing. ❧ Leominster, England

First published 1992 in the United States by
Wm. B. Eerdmans Publishing Co.,
255 Jefferson Ave. S.E., Grand Rapids, Michigan 49503,
and by Friendship Press,
475 Riverside Drive, Room 772, New York, N.Y. 10115,
and in Europe by Gracewing,
2 Southern Avenue, Leominster, HR6 0QF, UK.

Printed in the United States of America

Library of Congress Cataloging-in-Publication Data

Rienstra, Marchiene Vroon, 1941-
Swallow's Nest / Marchiene Vroon Rienstra.
p.   cm.
Includes bibliographical references.
ISBN 0-8028-0624-4 (pbk.)
1. Bible. O.T. Psalms — Devotional use. 2. Devotional exercises.
3. Bible — Prayers. I. Title.
BS1430.4.R54   1992
242'.2 — dc20   92-15807
                                 CIP

Friendship Press ISBN 0-377-00248-8
Gracewing ISBN 0 85244 214 9

The author and publisher gratefully acknowledge permission granted by
the publishers listed on page v to reprint copyrighted material.

Acknowledgments

The hymn prayer "Morning Glory, Starlit Sky," with words by W. H. Vanstone, is copyright © 1980 by J. W. Shore. Used by permission.

The hymn prayer "O Day of God, Draw Nigh in Beauty and in Power" is copyright © 1937 by R. B. Y. Scott. Used by permission.

In the hymn prayers, the versifications of Psalms 4, 5, and 141 are from the *Psalter Hymnal,* copyright © 1987, CRC Publications, Grand Rapids, MI 49560. Used by permission.

The material used in the appendix comes from four volumes:

Meditations with Hildegard of Bingen by Gabriele Uhlein, copyright © 1982. Used by permission of Bear & Co., Inc., P.O. Box 2860, Sante Fe, New Mexico 87504.

Meditations with Julian of Norwich by Brendan Doyle, copyright © 1983. Used by permission of Bear & Co., Inc., P.O. Box 2860, Sante Fe, New Mexico 87504.

Meditations with Mechtild of Magdeburg by Sue Woodruff, copyright © 1982. Used by permission of Bear & Co., Inc., P.O. Box 2860, Sante Fe, New Mexico 87504.

Meditations with Teresa of Avila by Camille Campbell, copyright © 1985. Used by permission of Bear & Co., Inc., P.O. Box 2860, Sante Fe, New Mexico 87504.

Note: If, inadvertently, we have not acknowledged a particular copyright, we offer sincere apologies and the assurance that the oversight will be rectified in subsequent printings.

This book is lovingly dedicated
to all the sisters of the Morning Star,
who seek, with me,
to transform our traditions,
so that we might be at home in them;
and to Julie, Elise, and the Morning Star "Sistery,"
who first prayed
these Psalms and prayers with me,
and encouraged me all the way!

Contents

Preface

I owe the inspiration for this book of psalm-prayers to three important sources.

The first source comes from my heritage and my family. Both the Christian Reformed and the United Presbyterian denominations in which I was raised have a strong tradition of psalm singing and reading. My grandparents on both sides, and my father as well, knew many Dutch psalm-songs by heart. We read from the Psalms at the table every noon, and I heard them sung in church every Sunday. We had psalters in our house and learned many psalms by singing them around the piano together as a family. They became so much a part of me that I took them for granted until, as an adult, I found myself in churches that used the Psalms only occasionally. Then how I missed them! I realized what a treasure they were, and how profoundly they had formed my spirit, my outlook on life, and my relationship with God.

Fortunately, I found a second rich psalm-source at St. Gregory's Episcopal Benedictine Monastery, which I visit regularly for days of retreat and renewal. The community of monks there taught me the contemplative and ecclesiastic dimensions of the Psalms — how they can be prayed against one's inner enemies of despair or confusion or doubt and the like, and how they voice the prayer of Christ and the church through the ages. As I entered into their 1500-year-old tradition of praying the Psalms seven times a day, I came to understand how the monks' act of frequently praying the same words of Scripture together created a profound sense of community among them. It also linked them in strong solidarity with the whole company of those who have also prayed the Psalms through the ages and throughout the world. I came to see that praying the Psalms was a vital way to experience the reality of the "communion of the saints."

Then I found a third psalm-source through my friendship with a number of Catholic Dominican nuns. In the middle of their busy lives of service, they faithfully follow the discipline of praying the Psalms morning, noon, and evening. From them I learned that the Psalms are a major reason for their passion for social justice and peace and their keen awareness of the suffering of others both near and far. Through their praying and living of the Psalms, I came to realize how filled the Psalms are with God's passion for justice for the poor and oppressed in every place. I experienced how praying the Psalms often can create a strong sense of solidarity with the suffering of others and help people move from an individual and parochial outlook to participation in God's great perspective.

My Dominican sisters also taught me to treasure the way the Psalms so honestly reflect the full range of human emotion — joy, sorrow, vengeful anger, despair, hope, doubt — all in Spirit-inspired words of prayer. When I struggled with some of the vengeful and violent language in the Psalms, they reminded me that expressing honest feelings to God in prayer in a spirit of open trust, while leaving vengeance in God's hands, was a healthy way to handle anger. And I saw that though many of the Psalms did not express my personal feelings on a given day, they certainly were expressing what others felt, and that I could thereby stretch my soul beyond my own personal experience. When I reflected on the injustice and hurt that so many experience, it seemed to me that the anger and pleading found in the Psalms was an appropriate response to the awful situations in which so many of my fellow human beings still live.

Best of all, the book of psalm-prayer used by the Dominican Sisters of Marywood introduced me to inclusive language for God and people. Its liberating effect inspired me to go one step further and paraphrase the Psalms in feminine language for God and people, in order to offer a badly needed balance to the male language for God and people that has so dominated the Christian tradition.

When I shared my first attempts at doing this with some other women, they were deeply moved. "This helps me really know and feel myself to be the womanly image of God!" one of them exclaimed. They enthusiastically supported the writing of this book. It is their conviction that there is a great healing potential for women and men in valuing and recovering the feminine aspect of God that has sustained me. It is their discovery that the Psalms, when expressed as the experience of women, provide a way of praying that empowers women and the feminine that has inspired me. It is their resonance with my experience and approach that has given me the support I needed.

I especially want to thank Lillian Sigal, my Jewish friend whose scholarly and friendly suggestions were of great value; Sharon Miller, whose steadfast interest and input were so important in the writing of this book; Ina Vondiziano, whose wise advice and patient support in the preparation of the book for publication were essential; Mary Hietbrink, whose editorial skill made this a better book; and John, my supportive and patient husband, whose love, understanding, and backing have made much more than this book possible!

Introduction

On the night my father died, as our family sat in stunned silence around his bed, my youngest brother took the Bible and began reading the Psalms, starting with Psalm 1. It is as good a description of my father as one could find anywhere, and it evoked tears of both grief and gratitude. With breaking voices, we passed the Bible around and, turn by turn, continued reading straight through the Psalms for a good while — a custom commonly practiced among Jews and Russian Orthodox Christians, who read the Psalms in the presence of the departed one from death until the funeral service, day and night, in shifts. We did not do that much, but we found new meaning in the Psalms as we read them together that night, with our father's life and faith in mind. It was an entirely fitting thing for us to do as Reformed Christians too, for he and we had been nurtured in the singing of the Psalms all our lives. We knew many of them by heart, set to music; and we keenly felt that we were praying them with him, and with myriads of other believers as well, around his deathbed in that little room in the nursing home.

I tell this story to say that from the very beginnings of the Christian church, its members have prayed the Psalms constantly, both in the relative calm of daily life and in crisis. They learned to do this from the Jewish tradition in which Christianity is so deeply rooted. And they passed on the practice through generations, long after the church and the synagogue had gone separate ways.

That is why the Psalms are often called "the prayer book of the Bible." Through them, the church through the centuries has taught her children to pray. The multitude of monastic communities throughout the ages and throughout the world, to this very moment, have prayed the Psalms every day. The Anglican and Episcopal traditions use them liberally in their liturgy for daily morning and evening prayer in the parish. The Reformed and Presbyterian tradition used to allow only the Psalms to be sung in public worship, and in the Catholic, Orthodox, and some Protestant churches, the Psalms still have prominence in worship. Christians of all kinds have found that they contain the essentials of faith and life, profound wisdom, and an expression of the whole range of human feeling in response to God. Jesus had them often on his lips, and the writers of the New Testament quote from them more frequently than any other part of the Old Testament.

When we pray them regularly and repeatedly, they enrich, enlarge, and shape our prayer, our souls, and our lives. They protect us from the unhealthy individualism and religious privatism of our society. They unite us in prayer with others in all ages and places, whose feelings and circumstances may not always be like ours but who nevertheless are one with us in faith. They create a deep unity of soul and solidarity of spirit as we pray them with the consciousness of the company of these others the world over. They make the communion of the saints that transcends time an experiential reality in our lives. When we pray them often, they become a treasury of spiritual resources upon which we can draw when our well runs dry.

While they have been spiritually nourishing to so many through the ages, the Psalms, like all of Scripture, have a masculine bias in their language and imagery for God and human experience. This, many scholars argue, is the result of the cultural conditioning that affected all the writers of the various books of the Bible. An essential and only recently noted aspect of this cultural conditioning is the patriarchal nature of the cultures that were the context in which Scripture was written. After all, though the Holy Spirit inspired the truths of Scripture, it is men who wrote as well as interpreted and applied the Scriptures, and so it is not surprising that women's point of view is barely visible! As a result, women and men have been deprived of the wisdom that women have to offer, and women have been wounded by the lack of esteem and attention they experience in the Christian tradition.

I believe that this is not the Holy Spirit's intent, and that the feminine dimension needs to be recognized and appreciated if we are to be led further into the truth by the Holy Spirit.

In order to enable myself and others to pray the Psalms in a way that emphasizes and celebrates the feminine aspects of God and of human nature and experience, I have paraphrased them, first consulting the Hebrew text and then making those changes in language and metaphor that reflect and nourish the feminine. I must emphasize that while I have tried to do this work sensitively and responsibly, my aim has been to provide not a text for scholarly study but rather a devotional rendering that I hope will enable readers to begin to appreciate and pray the Psalms in a new and enriching way.

I recognize that using feminine pronouns for God raises theological issues that are still a matter of considerable controversy within the Christian tradition. But I believe that the reader of this book can find value in it whether or not he or she believes that feminine pronouns for God have the same theological claim as do the masculine pronouns. The ground upon which I have ventured my paraphrase is simply the common affirmation on all sides that God finally is neither male nor female, but far more than both, and that God's nature includes qualities attributed to both male and female in varying ways in all cultures. I am furthermore convinced that psychologically the exclusive use of male language for God through the centuries can be balanced only by the use of female language for God, so that eventually believers will be able with both heart and head to relate to the "feminine" as well as the "masculine" face of God. My goal is not to replace masculine God-language with feminine God-language in the Christian tradition but to encourage the use of feminine language. For those who cannot get past the fact that Jesus called God "Father," I encourage at least thinking of the Holy Spirit in a feminine mode. Since Christians confess that the Three Persons are One, this is a way to restore the feminine to the Godhead.

My main concern is pastoral. At the one extreme there are those whose unfortunate relationship with fathers and other men makes it impossible to draw close to God imaged as father and male. And alternatively there are others whose unfortunate relationship with mothers and other women makes it impossible to draw close to God imaged as mother and female. Both images are needed so that believers may draw near to God as they are able and are given opportunity to recognize and withdraw their projections upon God, letting God be God — a Mystery of Love ultimately beyond all language and comprehension.

I have also created headings for many of the Psalms that encourage readers to imagine them as the prayers of particular women in a wide variety of circumstances all over the world. This provides a way of experiencing a strong solidarity through prayer with the particular joys, sorrows, and struggles of women. Thus the nourishing effect of praying the Psalms in feminine language is linked to a greater sense of compassionate union with the diverse lives of women, both in concrete and particular political and social contexts and in more universal kinds of experience. Placing the Psalms on the lips of particular women in this way opens up whole new levels of meaning and insight; one sees the appropriateness of the strong sentiments expressed in many of the Psalms. My hope, of course, is that beyond following my suggestions readers will be encouraged to imagine for themselves other women with whom they may sympathetically pray the Psalms.

Frequently I use the name "El Shaddai" for God, which is found often in the Old Testament and which can be translated from the Hebrew as "breasted God," since the root word in "Shaddai" means "female breast." This is a clearly feminine name for God that supports the female images for God which are present in Scripture.

Finally, I have substituted terms that make the Psalms less limited to Jewish history and geography and instead extend their implied meaning to make them more universal, more clearly applicable to inner as well as outer experience, and more descriptive of contemporary as well as ancient social contexts. In a more thorough-going way I have used more contemporary language where it was appropriate, and sometimes condensed a psalm or rearranged some of its parts. My goal has consistently been to give the Psalms fresh voice.

These features may make this book particularly valuable to women, that part of the body of Christ which has in significant ways been neglected. But I hope that these psalm-prayers will also be used to enrich and inspire gatherings of the whole body of Christ.

I have arranged the Psalms to be prayed three times a day — morning, noon, and night — since this was the ancient Jewish and Christian tradition. If they are used in this way, it is possible to pray through the psalter every four weeks. This allows for the kind of repetition which, over time, results in knowing the Psalms "by heart," in the profoundest sense of that telling phrase.

They are also arranged with a coordinating theme for each day, suggested either by Christian tradition, in the case of Friday and Sunday, or by more psychological reasons on the other days. "Hope," for example, seems a fitting theme for Monday, the start of a new week. Tuesday, when we may see clearly what the week will demand of us, seems a good day to seek and reflect on God's word and wisdom, which then leads to the faith and trust expressed in Wednesday's prayers. By Thursday, the week is growing old, and often a kind of weariness sets in. Difficulties loom larger. It seems an appropriate day for prayers calling for God's help and justice. Friday, of course, which recalls Christ's death on Good Friday, is an appropriate day for prayers lamenting suffering and confessing sin. Then we are ready on Saturday, our day of replenishment, to celebrate God's creating and creative acts, and on Sunday to remember with gratitude God's saving and redeeming deeds. Naturally, the themes are somewhat arbitrarily chosen, and not everything in each day's prayer reflects the theme, but the choosing of a theme helps provide a focus and a coherence that might otherwise be missing.

The Psalms are accompanied by hymns that echo the theme of the day or the time of the day (morning or evening) or both, in the voices of Christians of all kinds. They have come to us through the centuries after the Psalms were written, thus providing prayer that reflects the developing corporate prayer of the church. Where revision was necessary I have changed the language in these hymns to reflect the feminine aspects of divine and human nature that have received such scant attention in the church's hymnody.

While the hymns are largely from the treasury of Protestant worship, the opening sentences for morning, noon, and night and the prayers of the faithful at midday come from the treasury of the prayer of the whole church and of the Jewish faith as well, for "God's Spirit has not left herself without a witness" anywhere in the world! These prayers still further enlarge and enrich our prayer, and reveal the profound unity we share in our longing for and communion with the one true God of all people and places.

The readings from Scripture that are suggested for morning and evening prayer I have chosen to fit in some way with the day's theme and Psalms. In addition, either they are passages that acknowledge women's value in God's eyes and depict their contribution to salvation history, or they are passages which, if read with women in mind, encourage women to be all that God made and calls them to be. I recommend reading them in the New Revised Standard Version. I also encourage you as you read these passages to substitute feminine language for God and people where this seems appropriate and helpful.

There are many beautiful prayer litanies I might have borrowed from the liturgies of such churches as the Orthodox, the Catholic, and the Episcopal. They teach us to pray regularly not only for our own private concerns but also for the world, its leaders, our communities, the church, strangers, the sick and the needy, and the goals of peace and justice. I have tried to honor this lesson from these parts of the church by suggesting topics for prayer that cover the same ground, while at the same time honoring the Protestant "free church" tradition of spontaneous prayer in one's own words and way, expressed silently or aloud. Thus only the topics and not the words are suggested. Of course, they are meant not to limit what is prayed for but to suggest a regular planned basis for intercession which can then be expanded as the Spirit leads.

Finally, to accompany the Psalms, I have included an appendix of readings from four women theologians and mystics whose voices have seldom been heard until recently, although they have marvelous things to say. They are Hildegard of Bingen, Teresa of Ávila, Mechthild of Magdeburg, and Julian of Norwich. Their profoundly nurturing and feminine perspective enhances the Psalms and other prayers.

My hope is that this book will provide a nest of feminine prayer that will sustain and nurture many. (The word *feminine*, by the way, has often been defined by cultural stereotypes that I trust the contents of this book will effectively challenge.) As I have written its pages, I have felt like the swallow of the Psalms, building a nest of prayer on God's altar, where the feminine in me and other women — and also in men — can find a home.

How lovely are all the places of Your dwelling, El Shaddai!
My soul faints with longing for the beauty of Your presence.
My whole being shouts for joy to You, O living God!

Even the sparrow finds a home in Your presence,
and the swallow finds a place to build a nest for herself,
where she may also lay her young — on Your very altars,
    El Shaddai!

(Ps. 84:1-4)

My soul and the souls of many others long and faint for the feminine presence of God. This nest of Psalms, built on the altar of prayer, provides a place where our souls, like swallows, can sing for joy to the living God!

It seems important to make such a place available, because this kind of prayer, when engaged in often and wholeheartedly, changes consciousness and transforms people and the societies they create. Prayer that affirms, nourishes, and empowers the neglected and oppressed feminine in the human soul, in the church, and in society has the power and possibility of bringing about a much-needed healing and wholeness for humanity and the earth. It becomes an important way of making ourselves open to God's transforming grace, so that the will of God may be done more fully on earth as it is in heaven.

If this book contributes to that end in a way as small as a swallow's nest, my heart will be filled with joy!

—Marchiene Vroon Rienstra

Different Ways
to Use This Book

1. It can be used by individuals for private, personal prayer every day or occasionally.

2. It can be used by families or other groups.

3. Other readings can be substituted for the suggested ones, particularly if one is already following a lectionary or some other guided way of reading Scripture.

4. It can also be used in ways other than the given three-times-a-day, four-week pattern. For example, one could use it for prayer just once a day and take three months to move through it, using the morning prayers one month, the evening prayers another, and so on.

5. The morning and evening prayers can form the basis for a brief, simple worship service. A few other elements from among the following can be added: more hymns or songs; a period of silence; a meditation with words, music, art, or movement to accompany the reading; some form of offering and/or an "agape feast" of eating and drinking together in celebration of God's redemptive acts in Christ.

6. It can be used as a book of resources from which to borrow pieces to use in other settings and in other ways.

7. The Psalms can be read in such a way that they correspond to the liturgical seasons. (See the Liturgical Index.)

Week One

Sunday

Worshiping God Our Savior

MORNING PRAYER

Opening:

> This is the day our God has made!
> Let us be glad and rejoice in it!

Hymn Prayer:

> O day of rest and gladness, O day of joy and light,
> O balm for care and sadness, most beautiful, most bright!
> On thee the high and lowly through ages joined in tune,
> Sing holy, holy, holy to the great God Triune.
>
> On thee at the creation the light first had its birth,
> on thee, for our salvation, Christ rose from depths of earth;
> on thee our God most gracious the Spirit sent from heav'n,
> and thus on thee, most glorious, a triple light was giv'n.

Christopher Wordsworth, 1862
(text modified by author)

Psalm 5:1-8, 11-12
(This might be the prayer of a woman deacon.)

Listen to my cry, El Shaddai, and give ear to my inmost thoughts.
O my God and my friend, attend to me as I pour out my prayer before You.
I present myself to You at daybreak, for I know that every morning
You are there to hear my prayer.

I have confidence in You, because I know
that You are set against all wickedness.
I know that evil cannot survive in Your holy presence,
that self-important, self-righteous people
have no standing in Your eyes.
Neither can You abide those who are destructive of life.
You will wipe out all deceit, all lying, and all violence.

How glad I am that I can enter Your house
confident in the abundance of Your grace!
I will worship in Your Holy presence with fitting and reverent awe.

In spite of all obstacles, lead me in the justice of Your ways, El Shaddai.
Let Your paths be plain to me.

Let all who put their trust in You dance with joy and shout with gladness,
because Your love is their covering.
Let all who love You be joyful in You always,
For You, El Shaddai, will bless the upright in heart,
and surround them with the warm cloak of Your favor.

Psalm 15
(This might be the prayer of a woman judge.)

O God, who is able to live for You, and enjoy Your holy presence?
She who lives uprightly, works for justice, and speaks the truth;
she who does not revile others, or do evil to a friend,
        or harass her neighbor;
she who keeps company with others who love and revere God,
but avoids intimacy with those who ignore or forsake Her;
she who keeps her promises and lives with integrity;

4

she who lends money generously, without expecting interest,
and will not condemn the innocent.

She who lives this way will never be shaken.

Psalm 117
(This is the prayer of God's church.)

> Praise El Shaddai, all nations! Exalt God, all peoples!
> For great is Her steadfast love toward everyone!
> The faithfulness of El Shaddai endures forever.
> Alleluia!

Reading: Exodus 1:13-21 or selection from the Appendix

Prayer: Intercession for the local church

Benediction: May the strength of God, the Source of all Being,
the wisdom of God the Eternal Word,
and the joy of God the Holy Spirit abide with us always. Amen.

MIDDAY PRAYER

Opening:

> Our help is in the name of God,
> who gave birth to the earth and the heavens.

Psalm 9:1-12, 15-20
*(This might be the prayer of Russian women who
lived through the revolution against communism.)*

> We will give thanks to You, O God, with all our hearts.
> We will tell of Your wonderful acts as we rejoice and praise Your name.

In turning from You, our enemies stumbled backward and perished.
For You have always been behind what is right, and upheld our cause.
Your judgments are always just.
You rebuke the powerful, destroying the wicked among them.
You blot out their names forever.
Those who oppose You end up in everlasting ruin.
You root out their dwelling places, and they are forgotten.

But You, El Shaddai, shall reign forever.
You have established Your rule for the sake of justice everywhere.
You judge the whole world with uprightness, all the peoples with fairness.

God is a stronghold for the oppressed, their protection in troubled times.
All those who know Her goodness trust in Her,
for She has never forsaken anyone who put confidence in Her.

Sing praises to God, who dwells in the hearts of Her people!
Tell Her deeds among all people!
Remind them that She repays the violent and remembers the afflicted.
See how the unjust have sunk in the pit they dug.
Their own feet are caught in the trap they hid for others!
Meditate on this, and learn from it!

The wicked shall depart to the dwelling of the dead.
Nations that forget God shall all pass away.
But the needy shall not be forgotten;
the hope of the poor shall not perish.

God will arise and prevent the triumph of human pride.
Proud nations shall fall under Her judgment.
Their leaders shall learn to fear El Shaddai,
and realize their own mortality.

Psalm 116:1-14
*(This might be a woman's song of thanks
for recovery from a hard childbirth.)*

I love God, because She always hears my call for help.
Because She listens in love to me, I will call on Her as long as I live.

The cords of death choked me with distress,
and the threat of dying filled me with anguish.
Then I called to God, saying, "I beg You, El Shaddai, save my life!"

God was gracious and good to me, and in Her mercy saved me.
She preserves all the humble, and saves those, like me, who are desperate.
Now my soul is at rest in God's graciousness.
For She delivered me, body and soul, from death.
She tenderly wiped the tears from my eyes,
and kept me from falling into the pit of death.
Because of Her help, I now walk before Her face in the land of the living!

What shall I offer to El Shaddai for all Her goodness to me?
I will join in prayer in the presence of all Her beloved,
and with them lift up the cup of salvation,
and praise Her holy name. Alleluia!

Silence

Prayer of the Faithful:

Holy Spirit, all creation praises you.
Creation has life because of you.
You are precious salve for broken bones, for festering wounds.
You transform them to precious gems!
Now gather us together in Your praise.
Lead us on the proper path.
O Holy Spirit, Fiery Comforter Spirit,
Life of the life of all creatures,
Holy are You, You that give existence to all form.
Holy are You, You that are balm for the mortally wounded.
Holy are You, You that cleanse deep hurt.
Fire of love, breath of all holiness, You are so delicious to our hearts!
You infuse our hearts deeply with the good smell of virtue.
O Holy Spirit, clear fountain, in You we perceive God,
who gathers the perplexed and seeks the lost.
Bulwark of life, You are the hope of oneness for that which is separate.
You are the girdle of propriety, You are holy salvation.
Shelter those caught in evil, free those in bondage,
for the Divine Power wills it.

You are the mighty way in which every thing
that is in the heavens, on the earth, and under the earth,
is penetrated with connectedness, is penetrated with relatedness.
Holy Spirit, through you clouds billow, breezes blow,
stones drip with trickling streams,
streams that are the source of the earth's lush greening.
Likewise, You are the source of human understanding.
You bless with the Breath of Wisdom.
Thus, all of our praise is Yours, You who are the melody itself of praise,
the joy of life, the mighty honor,
the hope of those to whom You give the gifts of the Light. Amen.

Hildegard of Bingen, 1098-1179

Benediction: May God, the One who is the Lover and Savior of all, especially of those who believe, fill your being and each day with the blessedness of constant communion with Her and with all who love Her, now and forever. Amen.

EVENING PRAYER

Opening:

Let our prayer rise before You like incense,
and the lifting up of our hands be an evening sacrifice.

Hymn Prayer:

The day You gave us, God, is ended;
the darkness falls at Your behest.
To You our morning prayer ascended;
Your praise shall hallow now our rest.

We thank You that Your church, unsleeping
while earth rolls onward into light,
through all the world her watch is keeping,
and rests not now by day or night.

As o'er each continent and island
the dawn leads on another day,
the voice of prayer is never silent,
nor dies the strain of praise away.

So be it, God! Your rule shall never,
like earth's proud empires, pass away;
Your reign is here, and grows forever
till all Your creatures own Your sway.

John Ellerton, 1870
(text modified by author)

Psalm 84:1-7, 10-12

(This might be the prayer of a woman minister.)

How lovely are all the places of Your dwelling, El Shaddai!
My soul faints with longing for the beauty of Your presence.
My whole being shouts for joy to You, O living God!

Even the sparrow finds a home in Your presence,
and the swallow finds a place to build a nest for herself,
where she may also lay her young — on Your very altars, El Shaddai!
Blessed are all creatures who dwell in Your presence,
always singing Your praise!

And blessed are all the women who find their strength in You,
whose hearts are Your houses of worship.
As they go through the valley of weeping,
they turn it into a place of wellsprings.
Blessings shower on them like the spring rain.
Because they are able to see Your Holiness everywhere,
they go onward from strength to strength.

A day in Your presence, O God, is better than a thousand far from You.
I would rather serve You in small and humble ways
than live in luxury and power among the wicked.

You are a God of grace and glory, shielding and enlightening us.
You withhold nothing good from those who act justly.
El Shaddai, blessed is the woman who relies completely on You!

Psalm 16

(This might be the prayer of a devout elderly widow.)

I know You always watch over me, O God, and so I take refuge in You.
El Shaddai, it is You alone who are God, and the source of everything good.

I delight in the faithful in the land, whose lives radiate Your goodness.
The unfaithful who choose what is false multiply their sorrows.
I want no part of their life, nor will I choose what they value.
For You alone, O God, are the choice of my heart.
You are the One who determines my destiny.
In Your mercy You have placed me in pleasant circumstances,
and provided me with a precious heritage.

I bless El Shaddai, who gives me wise counsel,
and instructs my heart through the night.
Thus I am always mindful of Her presence.
With Her beside me, I shall not be shaken.

Therefore my heart is filled with gladness, and my soul with glory!
My body also rests safe and secure, knowing that God will not
     leave me in death
or allow Her beloved to experience corruption.
She constantly shows me the path of life.
In Her presence is unbounded joy;
at Her right hand are pleasures without end!

Reading: Exodus 2:1-10 and 15:20-21 or selection from the Appendix

Prayer: Intercession for the church worldwide, especially for its unity

Benediction: May God, like a mother eagle, spread the wings of Her love and
protection over us throughout this night, and forever. Amen.

Monday

Hoping in God Our Future

MORNING PRAYER

Opening:

This is the day our God has made!
Let us be glad and rejoice in it!

Hymn Prayer:

O day of God, draw nigh in beauty and in power;
come with thy timeless judgment now to match our present hour.

Bring to our troubled minds, uncertain and afraid,
the quiet of a steadfast faith, calm of a call obeyed.

Bring justice to our land, that all may dwell secure,
and finely build for days to come foundations that endure.

Bring to our world of strife thy sovereign word of peace,
that war may haunt the earth no more, and desolation cease.

O day of God, draw nigh, as at creation's birth;
let there be light again, and set thy judgments in the earth.

R. B. Y. Scott, 1937

Psalm 57

(This might be the prayer of a woman fighting
street gangs in her neighborhood.)

O God, show me mercy and love me steadfastly!
For my soul takes refuge in You.
I hide in the shadow of Your wings till calamity passes me by.

I cry to El Shaddai to fulfill Her saving purposes for me.
I trust Her to send help and save me in my distress.
Surely She will put to shame those who seek to crush me with violence.

I know God will rescue me with faithful love,
though I live in the midst of street gangs flaming with violence and lust
armed with guns and knives and words that wound.

They set a trap for me, and I was disspirited.
They dug a pit for me, but they have fallen into it themselves!

God be praised! Let Her glory fill the whole earth!

My heart is fixed on You, O God; my soul steadfastly clings to You.
Awake to beauty, my soul!
Take drum and guitar and sing to God with beautiful melodies.
I will arouse the dawn with my praises!
I will sing Your glory among all my neighbors, O God.
I will sing to You in the presence of everyone I know.

For Your lovingkindness is more spacious than the sky,
and Your faithfulness encompasses the heavens.

Alleluia! Let God's glory fill the whole earth!

Psalm 130

(This might be the prayer of a woman
who is depressed and anxious.)

Out of dark depths I cry to You, El Shaddai!
O God, listen to my pleas!

I could not stand before You, asking for mercy,
if You held my sins against me.
But You are generous in forgiving,
and for this I gratefully revere You.

I wait patiently for El Shaddai, and I hope in Her promises.
My soul watches for signs of Her presence more eagerly
than those who keep night-watch long for the morning.

Let everyone everywhere hope in El Shaddai!
For She is full of steadfast love and offers abundant freedom to all.
Indeed, She shall free all Her people from guilt and sin and bondage!

Reading: Isaiah 65:17-25 or selection from the Appendix

Prayer: Intercession for the members of the immediate family

Benediction: May the God of all hope fill your hearts with eager anticipation and firm confidence in all Her promises, which are being fulfilled through Jesus Christ by the power of the Holy Spirit. Amen.

MIDDAY PRAYER

Opening:

Our help is in the name of God,
who gave birth to the earth and the heavens.

Psalm 2
*(This might be the prayer of poor women
who are faithful to God.)*

Why this raging of the nations and vain plotting by their people?
Their rulers defy God's will, and the leaders conspire together
against El Shaddai and Her beloved, saying,
"Let us disregard God's commands, and break Her bonds of justice."

She who lives in heaven laughs and derides their proud plots.
Her Word resounds against them in righteous anger,
and Her fury at their injustice frightens them.
"I have chosen my own to rule," She says.
"I will set them in places of power."

The decree of God is this:
We are Her children, to whom She has given birth.
She promises that the nations will belong to us,
and that the earth shall be ours to its farthest reaches.
In Her might we shall break the oppressive strength of the powerful;
it will be dashed in pieces like a clay pot.

Therefore, O rulers, be wise and be warned!
O leaders of the earth, serve God with reverence.
With trembling humility kiss Her feet and bow to Her just demands,
lest She be angry with you and you perish in your pride.
For Her wrath is an instrument of justice.

Blessed are all who take refuge in the strength of El Shaddai!

Psalm 76:1-9
*(This might be the prayer of women struggling
for peace in the Middle East.)*

God's people know Her well.
They know that She dwells where there is peace.
They know that Her abode in the land makes it holy.

Therefore, She destroys the flashing missiles that desecrate the land.
She breaks the tanks, the guns, the weapons of war.
The soldiers are stripped of their spoil and sink into everlasting sleep.
The warriors can no longer use their military might.
By the rebuke of the God of all mothers,
both pilot and fighter-plane are grounded.

How full of terror She is when Her righteous anger is aroused!
Then who can stand before Her, no matter what their power?
From heaven She utters just judgments.

The earth is expectant and still as God rises to establish Her peace,
granting justice to all the oppressed.

Silence

Prayer of the Faithful:

O God, give us a mind that is humble, quiet, peaceable, patient, charitable;
and a taste of your Holy Spirit in all our thoughts, words, and deeds.
O Lord, give us a lively faith, a firm hope, a fervent charity,
    and a love of you.
Take from us all lukewarmness in meditation and dullness in prayer.
Give us fervor and delight in thinking of you,
your grace, and your tender compassion toward us.
Give us, good God, the grace to work for the things we pray for!

Sir Thomas More, 1478-1535

Benediction: May the grace of God, the Source of all being; the love of Christ,
the Savior of all; and the comfort of the Holy Spirit fill our hearts
with hope, now and forever. Amen.

EVENING PRAYER

Opening:

Let our prayer rise before You like incense,
and the lifting up of our hands be an evening sacrifice.

Hymn Prayer:

From Thee all skill and science flow, all pity, care, and love;
all calm and courage, faith and hope; O pour them from above.

And give them, God, to each and all, as each and all shall need,
to rise like incense, each to Thee, in noble thought and deed.

And hasten, God, that perfect day when pain and death shall cease,
and Thy just rule shall fill the earth with health, and light, and peace.

Charles Kingsley, 1871

Psalm 85
(This might be the prayer of Palestinian and Jewish women.)

There was a time, O God, when You favored this land,
and restored the fortunes of Your people.
You forgave their wrongdoing and pardoned all their sin.
You withdrew Your wrath, and Your hot indignation cooled.

Restore us again, O God of our salvation.
Why are You still angry with us? How long will Your anger persist?
Will it last through all generations?
Revive us again, that we, Your people, may find joy in You!
Show us Your steadfast love, O God, and make us whole and holy.

Listen with me while El Shaddai speaks —
She speaks peace to Her people, to the faithful,
to those who return to Her with heartfelt repentance.
All who are devoted to Her will surely and soon be free,
free to dwell in a land once more filled with Her beauty and bounty.

Let lovingkindness and truthfulness meet!
Let mercy and honesty embrace one another!
Let faithfulness spring like grass from the earth,
and justice rain down from the sky.
Let righteousness make a way for Her,
and integrity a path for Her feet.

El Shaddai, be good to us.
Then our land will be fruitful and peaceful again.

Psalm 126
*(This might be the prayer of women who have struggled long
years for freedom in Eastern Europe and the Soviet Union.)*

When God restored our fortunes, it seemed too good to be true.
Then laughter filled our mouths, and we sang songs of joy.
Seeing our delight, those watching us said,
"God has done great things for them."
God has indeed done great things for us!
Great is our gladness!

O God, keep restoring our fortunes, like streams watering the desert!
May all those who sow in tears soon reap with shouts of joy!
May she who has gone forth weeping, bearing seed for sowing,
come home rejoicing, bringing in the sheaves of harvest.

Reading: Isaiah 11:1-9 or selection from the Appendix

Prayer: Prayer for the extended family

Benediction: May God, the Source of all hope, encouragement, and comfort,
be with us through the night and into the dawn of a new day. Amen.

Tuesday

Seeking God's Wisdom

MORNING PRAYER

Opening:

> This is the day our God has made!
> Let us be glad and rejoice in it!

Hymn Prayer:

> Behold, the morning sun begins its glorious way;
> its beams through all the nations run, and life and light convey.
>
> How perfect is Your word! And all Your judgments just!
> Forever sure Your Promise, God, in which we surely trust.
>
> I hear Your word with love, and I would fain obey;
> send Your good Spirit from Your heart to guide me lest I stray.

Isaac Watts, 1719

Psalm 1
(This might be in praise of a godly mother or grandmother.)

> Blessed is the woman who ignores the advice of the wicked,
> who avoids all the ways of sinners,

who refuses to sit with the scornful.
She delights instead in the will of God.
She muses on God's word day and night.

She is like a tree planted by rivers of water,
fruitful in season, with unwithered leaves.
She prospers in everything she does.

But the wicked are nothing like her.
They are like chaff which the wind blows away.
They cannot stand in the face of judgment;
they cannot remain among the righteous.
El Shaddai establishes the ways of the just,
but the way of the unjust shall surely perish.

Psalm 49
*(This might be the prayer of an exploited woman farming
land owned by rich "absentee landowners.")*

Listen to this, everyone — rich and poor, powerful and powerless,
    women and men the world over!
My mouth speaks wisdom, my tongue the truth,
because my heart is filled with God-given understanding.

I will not be afraid in evil days when oppression threatens me.
What of those who trust in their ill-gotten gain, who boast
    of their great wealth?
Can they pay God off and so save themselves from death?
Can their riches ransom them from the grave?

Indeed, no one can escape death's decay.
Even the lives of the wise end in death.
Everyone must perish and leave their wealth to others.

The grave is the eternal home of the rich,
the dwelling they are heir to.
How stupid to name lands as their own,
as if they would always belong to them!
No one will remain rich and powerful.
All are like the animals that weaken and die.

The fate of those who foolishly trust in their wealth,
of those who are are pleased by the folly they mouth,
is to enter into Sheol, like sheep, where death shall be their shepherd.
The pit of hell becomes their home.

But God will ransom my life from the power of death.
She shall surely take me home to Herself!

I will not be afraid, therefore, of people who are powerful and rich.
Though their wealth increases, it will not profit them when they die.
Their importance in this world will not last.
Though they enrich themselves at the expense of others,
and are praised for their power and wealth,
they will end up like others before them who did not see the light.
People who are rich in money and influence,
      but are poor in understanding —
they are like the beasts of the field that perish.
They will soon be cut off from life.

Reading: 1 Kings 22:8-20 or selection from the Appendix

Prayer: Intercession for friends and neighbors

Benediction: May God, the Giver of all wisdom, beauty, and well-being,
bless all who love Her with these gifts,
and grant that Her blessings may be generously shared. Amen.

MIDDAY PRAYER

Opening:

Our help is in the name of God,
who gave birth to the earth and the heavens.

Psalm 37

*(This might be the prayerful advice of nuns and other
women working in Latin American slums.)*

Do not fret yourself over evildoers
or envy the prosperity of the perverse.
They will soon wither like grass, fade away like cut flowers.

Instead, trust in God and do good.
Live in the land and feed on Her faithfulness.
If you delight yourself in God,
She will give you the desires of your heart.
If you put your burdens on God's shoulders,
She will act on your behalf.
She will make your integrity shine like the daylight,
your beauty glow like the moon and the sun.

Rest in El Shaddai, and wait patiently for Her to act.
Do not worry if evil seems to prosper in the world.
Abstain from constant rage, and do not let fury consume you.
You are the one who will be hurt most if you hold on to your anger.

Be sure that all who oppress others will be cut off.
But those who patiently wait on God will surely inherit the earth!
Wickedness will last only a little while longer.
Then you will look for it, and it will be gone.
It is the poor in spirit who will inherit the earth,
     who will be blessed with plenty and peace.

It is true that evildoers hate those who work for justice.
They threaten them with violence.
But God laughs at the unjust,
knowing their day of reckoning is coming!
The wicked wield their power to crush the poor and needy,
to slaughter those who work for justice.
But their own violence shall descend on their heads,
and their power shall soon be broken.

It is far better to have little and live justly
than to be rich and wicked.

For the wicked will be overthrown,
but God will uphold the righteous.

God acknowledges the lives of the just,
blessing them with an enduring heritage.
They survive evil times; they are strengthened even in famine.
But those who oppose El Shaddai are like the passing beauty of meadows.
They are like smoke disappearing into thin air.

Have you noticed how the unjust take advantage of others,
how they borrow without paying back?
But those with integrity give generously.
They are the people God blesses; they will inherit the land.
But those whom God opposes will lose whatever they possess.

The steps of women and men who live with integrity
are guided by God, who takes great delight in their ways.
Though they fall, they will rise again,
for El Shaddai takes hold of their hands.

Silence

Prayer of the Faithful:

My Lord and God,
the words of Your Spirit are laden with delights.
As often as I hear them, my soul seems to absorb them
and they enter the heart of my body like the most delicious food,
bringing unbounded joy and unspeakable comfort.

After hearing Your words, I remain both satisfied and hungry —
satisfied, for I desire nothing else;
but hungry, for I crave more of Your words.

St. Bridget of Sweden, 1302-1373

Benediction: May God, who is our Truth; Christ, who is God's Word made flesh;
and the Holy Spirit, who is our wisdom, lead us in the way of life
everlasting, this day and forever. Amen.

EVENING PRAYER

Opening:

Let our prayer rise before You like incense,
and the lifting up of our hands be an evening sacrifice.

Hymn Prayer:

Now comes the day's end as the sun is setting,
mirror of daybreak, pledge of resurrection;
while in the heavens choirs of stars appearing hallow the nightfall.

Therefore we come now evening rites to offer,
joyfully chanting holy hymns to praise You;
with all creation joining hearts and voices, singing your glory.

Give heed, we pray You, to our supplication,
that You may grant us pardon for offenses,
strength for our weak hearts, rest for aching bodies, soothing the weary.

Mozarabic hymn, 10th century

Psalm 92
(This might be the prayer of a woman music teacher.)

I love to offer You thanks, O God, and sing praise to Your name.
I love to proclaim Your love in the morning
and Your faithfulness every night
with stringed instruments and sweet-sounding melodies.
Your deeds gladden my heart,
and I dance for joy at the works of Your hands!

How great are Your works, El Shaddai!
How deep are Your designs!
The foolish and brutish do not see what I know —
though the wicked sprout up like grass, and evil flourishes everywhere,
they are doomed to eternal destruction.
But You are with us in every generation.

You give me the power and energy of a lioness;
You anoint me with the fragrant oil of Your blessing.
I will watch my enemies fall;
My assailants, I know, will meet their doom.

Upright women shall endure, like olive trees,
    shall grow great like mountain cedars.
Planted in the presence of God, they flourish in Her presence.
They still are fruitful in old age; they are green and full of sap.
They reveal the goodness and justice of the God who is their Rock.

Psalm 101:1-7

(This might be the prayer of a homemaker.)

When I sing of You, El Shaddai, I sing of mercy and justice.
I want to praise You, and learn to act wisely,
following Your wholesome ways.
Will You come and dwell in me?

I will walk with integrity of heart within my household.
I will not regard anything that is worthless or base.
I will reject the way of those who stray from Your paths.
I will not let myself be trapped by falsehood.
I will give no place to perversity.
I will shun all that is evil.
I will not listen to those who slander others.
I will not endure the arrogant or give heed to the overbearing.
I will favor the faithful in the land and live in communion with them.
My companions will be those who work for justice for all.
I will not support the telling of lies.
No deceit shall dwell in my house or in my heart.

Reading: Luke 2:36-38 or selection from the Appendix

Prayer: Intercession for enemies/adversaries/competitors

Benediction: May the love of God watch over you;
        may the peace of Christ fill your heart;
        may the presence of the Holy Spirit fill your sleep
        and speak in your dreams. Amen.

Wednesday

Trusting in God Our Refuge

MORNING PRAYER

Opening:

This is the day our God has made!
Let us be glad and rejoice in it!

Hymn Prayer:

Awake, my soul, and with the sun your daily stage of duty run;
shake off your sleep, and joyful rise to pay your morning sacrifice.

By influence of the Light Divine let your own light in good work shine;
reflect all heaven's gracious ways in ardent love and cheerful praise.

God, I my vows to You renew; scatter my sins as morning dew;
guard my first springs of thought and will, and with Yourself my spirit fill.

Direct, control, suggest this day all I design or do or say,
that all my pow'rs with all their might in Your sole glory may unite.

Thomas Ken, 1695

Psalm 23

(This might be the prayer of a woman who, though surrounded by difficulties, is at peace in the arms of God.)

Because El Shaddai shepherds me, my deepest needs are met.
She gives me rest in the green pastures of Her Word.
She leads me beside the still waters of prayerful silence.
She restores me, body and soul.
She leads me in the paths of wholeness.

Even when I walk in the shadow of death,
I need fear no evil, for She is with me.
Her rod and staff uphold and guide me.

She sets Her table before me in the presence of my inner enemies.
She anoints my head with the oil of Her blessing.
My cup of joy overflows!

I know that Her goodness and mercy will follow me as long as I live,
and that I will dwell forever in the house of Her loving presence.

Psalm 103

(This might be the celebratory prayer of a woman who has recently discovered God's love for her.)

El Shaddai, with all my soul, and all that is within me,
I bless Your holy name.
I remember with joy all Your blessings.
You forgive all my sin and heal all my dis-eases.
You save my life from ruin and crown me with lovingkindness.
You surround me with tender mercy and satisfy my desires with good.
As long as I live, You will renew my strength like the eagle's.

You always act with justice and vindicate all the oppressed.
You made Yourself known to Miriam and Moses,
and revealed Yourself through Your saving acts to all Your people.
You are merciful and gracious, slow to anger, and steadfast in love.
You seldom chasten and never remain angry.

You do not deal with us as our sin deserves;
You do not return what our bad behavior merits.
Your love is as high as the heavens are above the earth.
You remove our sinfulness from us as far as the east is from the west!
As a mother's heart embraces all her children,
So your great womb-love extends to all the faithful.

You know how fragile our bodies are, El Shaddai.
They so quickly return to the dust! Our days are like fast-fading grass.
We flourish for a little while like wildflowers in the fields.
When the wind blows over them, they wither and die.

But Your steadfast love, El Shaddai, lasts forever.
You pour out Your generosity on Your children — on all who revere You,
and all the generations of those who keep covenant with You.

Heaven and earth are Your home, and Your reign extends over all.
With all the angels and powers of heaven and earth,
we bless You, El Shaddai, and hasten to listen to the voice of Your Word.
All Your works in all places of Your dominion bless You, O God.

O my soul, bless El Shaddai!

Reading: Isaiah 49:13-16 or selection from the Appendix

Prayer: Intercession for the local community, town, or city

Benediction: May we enjoy the rich nourishment of God's wisdom and the safe-keeping of Her love, this day and always. Amen.

MIDDAY PRAYER

Opening:

Our help is in the name of God,
who gave birth to the earth and the heavens.

Psalm 11

(This might be the prayer of an abused woman against her inner enemies — despair, fear, a sense of worthlessness.)

How can you say to my soul, "Fly away, like a bird, to the mountains"?
There is no easy escape from the inner attacks of darkness.
The arrows of fear pierce my heart.
The foundation of my self-esteem is destroyed.
How can I be upright, or do what I need to do?

Yet God is within my body, which is Her holy temple.
She also dwells in the heavens and sees us, tests us all.
Though She lets those with integrity endure many trials,
Her soul hates those who love violence.

She will send fire and brimstone and a scorching wind
to destroy the despair that attacks me.
For God is loving and just, and always does what is right.
Those who act with integrity shall surely behold Her face.

Psalm 13

(This might be the prayer of a homeless young girl living on the streets.)

O my God, will You forget me forever?
Will You always hide Your face from me?
How long must I bear this pain in body and soul?
How long will I grieve night and day?
How long will my captors keep their power over me?

Answer me, El Shaddai! For You are my only hope.
Bring me into the light, lest I sleep in death.
Do not let my enemies overcome my resistance
or take more advantage of my weakness.

Without Your steadfast love I would die.
My heart keeps hoping for Your saving grace.
Even now, I will sing to You in my heart
and place all my hope in Your rescue.

Silence

Prayer of the Faithful:

O Heart of Love, I place all my trust in You.
I fear all things from my own weakness,
but I hope for all things from Your goodness.

St. Marguerite-Marie Alacoque, 1647-1690

Benediction: May you always take refuge under the sheltering wings of God, whose love overshadows all our days; and may You be blessed with the capacity to trust in Her goodness, whatever happens. Amen.

EVENING PRAYER

Opening:

Let our prayer rise before You like incense,
and the lifting up of our hands be an evening sacrifice.

Hymn Prayer:

All praise to Thee, my God, this night for all the blessings of the light;
throughout the night my spirit sings beneath Thy loving, outstretched wings.

Forgive me, God, as Thy dear one, the ill that I this day have done;
that with the world, myself, and Thee, I, ere I sleep, at peace may be.

O may my soul in Thee repose, and may sweet sleep my eyelids close;
sleep that may me more vig'rous make to serve Thee, God, when I awake.
Amen.

Thomas Ken, 1695
(text modified by author)

Psalm 3

(This might be the prayer of a black South African woman in the townships.)

O God, my enemies multiply in number.
So many keep coming against me!
They scornfully say, "God will never save her!"

But You, O God, are my wall of protection.
I glory in You, and in Your strength hold my head high.
I cry loudly to You, and You answer me.

I lie down and sleep in safety.
You keep watch over me until I wake again.
In spite of the violent people who surround me,
I am not afraid, nor faint-hearted.
I know that You will rise up and save me, breaking the power of violence.

Salvation belongs to You, El Shaddai!
Your blessing abides with Your people.

Psalm 4

(This might be the prayer of a woman worker suffering sexual harassment.)

When I call, answer me, O God of my integrity!
Deliver me from my distress!
Have mercy on me and hear my prayer.

O men, how long will you try to destroy my dignity?
How long will you assault me with lust and continue to live a lie?
Know that God protects Her daughters!
She hears when I call out for help!
Stop sinning, and repent with fear and trembling.
Consult the depths of your own hearts in sacred silence.
Offer to God the sacrifices of integrity and respect for all.

Many women say, "Who can do us any good?"
Let the light of Your face shine upon us, O God.

You fill my heart with a joy that is greater
than the pleasure of those stuffed with the best food and drink.
In peace I will lie down and sleep.
For in You, El Shaddai, I dwell in safety.

Reading: Hosea 11:1-4 or selection from the Appendix

Prayer: Intercession for the larger community: state, province, nation, etc.

Benediction: May God surround you this night and always with Her protection, faithfulness, and comfort. Amen.

Thursday

Crying Out to God for Justice

MORNING PRAYER

Opening:

This is the day our God has made!
Let us be glad and rejoice in it!

Hymn Prayer:

Let the whole creation cry, "Glory be to God on high!"
Heav'n and earth, awake and sing, unto God glad praises bring.
Praise Her, all ye hosts above, ever bright and fair in love;
Sun and moon, lift up your voice, night and stars, in God rejoice!

Men and women, young and old, raise the anthem manifold,
and let children's happy hearts in this worship bear their parts;
from the north to southern pole, let the mighty chorus roll:
"Holy, holy, holy One, glory be to God alone!"

Stopford A. Brooke, 1881
(text modified by author)

Psalm 12
(This might be the prayer of a woman in
politics advocating for the poor.)

Help us all, El Shaddai, for the godly cease to exist!
The faithful fade and fail among this people.
It seems that everyone speaks falsely with their neighbors,
with flattering lips and dishonest hearts.

God will silence all flattering lips, still all lying tongues —
all those who say, "Who has any say over us?
We shall say what we like, and prevail!"
God says, "I will now arise, because of the pain of the poor and the needy.
I will give them the well-being they long for."
These words of God are like pure silver, refined in the fire seven times.
She shall preserve the poor and guard them forever
from this hard-hearted generation.

Psalm 54
(This might be the prayer of a woman
who was the victim of slander.)

O God, save me and defend me with Your power.
Hear my prayer, O God, and listen to my cries of desperation.
For detractors have risen against me, cruel people who seek to wound me.
They have no regard whatever for You.

Look! God IS a helper to me! She is with those who cherish me.
She will bring my attackers to ruin, will destroy my enemies.

Gladly I offer You praise and thanksgiving, O God, for You are very good!
You deliver me from trouble and let me see the fall of my foes.

Reading: Luke 18:1-8 or selection from the Appendix

Prayer: Intercession for one's own country and its leaders

Benediction: May the tenderness of God, before whose face the guardian angels
of children always stand; the playfulness of the Holy Christ Child;
and the creative power of the Holy Spirit bless us throughout this
day and always. Amen.

MIDDAY PRAYER

Opening:

> Our help is in the name of God,
> who gave birth to the earth and the heavens.

Psalm 7

*(This might be the prayer of a woman living
in a ghetto of an American city.)*

> In You, El Shaddai, I seek refuge!
> Save me from those who harass me; deliver me from their cruelty.
> Like wild beasts, they threaten to rip me apart and wound me.
> Then who will rescue me?
> My God, what have I done to deserve this evil?
> If I myself have done what is wrong,
> if I have ever wronged my friends or even hurt my foes without cause,
> then I might deserve to have these men surround me
> and trample me into the ground, grinding my dignity to dust.
>
> Arouse Yourself, O God! Let Your anger destroy the violence of my foes.
> Exercise Your judgment against them on my behalf!
> Return to Your rightful place in our midst and gather us all around You!
> O God, You judge everyone fairly.
> Judge me by my upright deeds and the integrity within me.
>
> O let the evil of the wicked cease,
> but establish and support the just,
> You who try the minds and hearts of us all in fairness and righteousness.
>
> God is my protector, and the most just of judges.
> Therefore She is indignant with evildoers every day!
> If they do not repent, She will destroy their evil with deadly power.
>
> Look at these wicked people who give themselves to violence,
> who make mischief and breed falsehood.
> See how they fall into the trap they have made for others!
> Their violence returns upon their own heads,
> and they suffer the mischief they make.

Therefore, I will give thanks to God for Her justice and fairness.
I will always sing praise to the name of El Shaddai.

Psalm 140

*(This might be the prayer of women working
for peace in places where there is civil war.)*

O God, save us soon from the evil of violent people!
From their hatred and warfare deliver us!
With hateful hearts they devise plans for fighting;
all the day long they plan warfare.
They speak to each other deceitfully, with the forked tongue of a snake.
Their lips drip with an adder's poison.

Protect us from their hands, O God.
Preserve us from the traps they set.
With animosity they try to catch us in the web of their deceit.

El Shaddai, give ear to our urgent pleas!
O God, be our strong deliverer, and shield us in the day of violence.
Do not grant the warring wicked success in their plans;
frustrate their violent plots!

Those who surround us are stubborn and proud.
Let the mischief they make backfire on them!
Make burning coals of frustration fall on their heads!
Let them trip in their own traps and never rise to make war again!
Do not let those who plan attacks gain a foothold in our land.
Let peacemakers overcome the violent!

We pray in the confidence that You uphold the cause of all the afflicted.
We know You execute justice for the needy.
Therefore the upright shall give thanks to Your name,
and the peaceful shall rejoice in Your presence.

Silence

Prayer of the Faithful:

> O eternal Light, shine into our hearts.
> O eternal Goodness, deliver us from evil.
> O eternal Power, be our strength.
> O eternal Wisdom, dispel the darkness of our ignorance.
> O eternal Pity, show mercy to us.
> Grant that we may ever seek Your face with all our hearts,
>   minds, and strength.
> And in Your infinite mercy enable us to practice Your Holy Presence.

Alcuin, c. 732-804

Benediction: May the God who is our source of blessing, salvation, and power bless us this day and keep us close to Her heart. Amen.

EVENING PRAYER

Opening:

> Let our prayer rise before You like incense,
> and the lifting up of our hands be an evening sacrifice.

Hymn Prayer:

> O God, come quickly; hear me pray with lifted hands at close of day.
> May all my evening prayers arise like incense from the sacrifice.
>
> Guard lips and heart, without, within, so that I do not relish sin.
> God, let my footsteps never stray where evildoers point the way.
>
> O righteous God, Your chastisement, through friend or foe, in love is sent.
> Though grievous, it will profit me; a healing ointment it will be.
>
> Keep me from traps the sinful set; may they be caught in their own net.
> Though I am burdened and distressed, I look, O God, to You for rest.

From Psalm 141, put into verse by Marie J. Post, 1985
(text modified by author)

Psalm 141

*(This might be the prayer of an inner-city girl
struggling to resist the pressure to join a gang of drug dealers.)*

El Shaddai, when I cry, come quickly to me!
Listen to the pleas of my heart.
I offer my prayer, like incense, before You.
I lift up my hands as an evening sacrifice.

O God, guard my mouth and keep watch at the door of my lips.
Keep my heart from turning to destruction.
Keep me from joining others in their evil.
Prevent me from loving their luxuries.

Let me mercifully bless them with righteous rebuke.
Hear my continual prayer against their wicked deeds.
When they come to judgment for their evil,
may they know that my words were for their good.

Their deeds will be found out, like bones scattered at the mouth of hell.
When a plow furrows the earth, they are uncovered.

But my eyes look to You, El Shaddai, and in You I seek my safety.
Do not let my soul be vulnerable to them.
Keep me from the trap their hands have laid for me,
from the snares of these evildoers.
While the wicked fall into their own nets, let me escape unharmed.

Psalm 17

*(This might be the prayer of a woman refugee
arrested while seeking sanctuary.)*

El Shaddai, hear my cry, and defend the justice of my case!
Hear my prayer, for my lips are free from deceit.
You alone see what is right; reveal my integrity and justice.
If You test my heart, if You visit me in the night,
if You try me, You will find no corruption.

Keeping Your Word has kept me from falling into violence.
Because I have walked in Your tracks, my feet have never slipped.

When I call on You, will You answer me, O God of my life?
Will You lend me Your ear and hear me out?
O Savior of all who trust in You, show me Your marvelous love.
Save me with Your right hand from all who act unjustly.

Show me that You treasure me. Keep me as the apple of Your eye.
Hide me in the shadow of Your wings from those who seek to strip me,
the enemies of my body and soul who encircle me with danger.

They are fat with pride, and their mouths are full of arrogance.
With their eyes on my trail, they tracked me down.
They surrounded me like wild beasts eager for prey,
like animals hiding in ambush.

Arise, El Shaddai! Confront them with Your power!
Deliver me from them, and overthrow their plans for me.
From those who are greedy and proud deliver me,
O God of my salvation.
May their stomachs be stuffed with your recompense;
may their children lose their inheritance.

As for me, I will be satisfied when I see Your face mirrored in justice;
and when, with perfect integrity, I finally awake with Your likeness.

Reading: Luke 13:10-17 or selection from the Appendix

Prayer: Intercession for other countries, their leaders, and their welfare

Benediction: May the God of justice and mercy unite us in compassionate solidarity with all those in need, that our lives may be just and merciful, and a source of Her blessing to many. Amen.

Friday

Confession and Lamentation before God

MORNING PRAYER

Opening:

This is the day our God has made!
Let us be glad and rejoice in it!

Hymn Prayer:

Come, let us to our loving God with contrite hearts return;
our God is gracious, nor will leave the desolate to mourn.

Long has the night of sorrow reigned; the dawn shall bring us light:
God shall appear, and we shall rise with gladness in Her sight.

Our hearts, if God we seek to know, shall know Her and rejoice;
Her coming like the morn shall be, like morning songs Her voice.

As dew upon the tender herb, diffusing fragrance round,
as showers that usher in the spring, and cheer the thirsty ground,

so shall Her Presence bless our souls, and shed a joyful light,
that hallowed morn may chase away the sorrows of the night.

John Morison, 1781
(text modified by author)

39

Psalm 22

(This might be the prayer of a Jewish woman
who finally escaped a Nazi death-camp.)

O my God, why have You abandoned me?
Why are You so distant from the sound of my groaning?
Why do You fail to save me?
Every day I call, but You do not answer.
Every night I cry, but You are silent.

Yet my people have always praised You for Your holiness.
When they trusted in You, You always delivered them.
When they cried to You, You came to their rescue again and again.
When they put their confidence in You, You never let them down.

But I feel as if I were more worm than human.
I am despised and scorned by everyone around me.
My captors deride me, shaking their heads and mocking me:
"She trusted in God. If God truly delights in her, let God rescue her!"

I know You as the One who took me from the womb.
You cradled me upon my mother's breasts.
From my birth I have been cast upon You.
Since my mother bore me, You alone have been my God.
Do not forsake me now that I am in trouble, with no one else to help!

I am surrounded by guards who look like strong bulls.
Their mocking mouths are like the jaws of ravenous beasts.
My bones are pulled apart, and my limbs are like water.
My hearts melts within me like hot wax.
My strength is dried up like baked and broken pottery.
My tongue clings to my jaws.
Is it You who lay me in the dust of death?

Evildoers surround me like dogs, piercing my hands and feet.
I am so starved I can count all my bones.
See how they stare at me!
They gamble over my clothing, dividing it among them.

O God, do not be so far away. Help me! Hurry to my rescue!
Deliver my soul from their attacks, my body from their assaults!
Save me from their devouring mouths, their evil threats and thrusts.

El Shaddai! You have answered me! . . .

I will proclaim Your saving grace to all my sisters and brothers.
I will praise You among the assembly of the faithful!

All you children of my people, glorify God, and stand in awe before Her!
For El Shaddai has not ignored the suffering of the afflicted.
She has not turned away from the cries of those in pain.

You, O God, are the theme of my praise in the congregation of Your people.
I will pay my vows before those who revere You.
Now I know that the starved shall eat and be satisfied.
All suffering seekers will someday praise You!
May their hearts live forever!

All the ends of the earth shall remember and return, O God, to You!
All the families of the nations shall worship before You, El Shaddai!
For to You belongs true dominion; Your reign reaches to the ends
      of the earth.
All the wealthy, all the poor, all those ground down in the dust —
together they will worship before You.
Their children shall also serve You, and tell the next generation,
who in turn will proclaim Your deliverance to a people yet unborn:
"Hear the great things God has done for us!"

Reading: Luke 4:14-21 or selection from the Appendix

Prayer: Intercession for the world and for justice and mercy for its women

Benediction: May God bless us with forgiveness for our sins, reconciliation with those from whom we are divided, and solidarity with all who suffer. Amen.

MIDDAY PRAYER

Opening:

> Our help is in the name of God,
> who gave birth to the earth and the heavens.

Psalm 14
(This might be the prayer of a
black woman preacher.)

> Only fools say in their hearts, "There is no God!"
> They act corruptly and do hateful deeds.
> In fact, they never do anything good!
>
> From heaven God looks at these fools to see if any act wisely,
> to see if any seek after Her.
> But they all have gone astray; every one of them is corrupt.
> There are none whose lives are good — not even one!
>
> Evildoers who devour the poor like bread know nothing at all;
> they never call upon God.
> But they will shake with fear when they see that God sides with the upright.
> Though they try to dash the hopes of the poor, God does not permit it.
>
> It is God's people who will lead the way to salvation!
> When God finally restores all things, how great will be our rejoicing!

Silence

Prayer of the Faithful:

> O God, from You flows true and continual kindness.
> You had cast us off, and justly so,
> but in Your mercy You forgave us.
> You were at odds with us, and You reconciled us.
> You had set a curse on us, and You blessed us.
> You had banished us from the garden, and You called us back again.

You took away the fig leaves that had been an unsuitable garment,
and You clothed us in a cloak of great value.
You flung wide the prison gates,
and You gave the condemned a pardon.
You sprinkled clean water on us, and You washed away the dirt.

St. Gregory of Nyssa, c. 335-394

Benediction: May God's mercy mark all our ways,
and make us bearers of the same divine mercy. Amen.

EVENING PRAYER

Opening:

Let our prayer rise before You like incense,
And the lifting up of our hands be an evening sacrifice.

Hymn Prayer:

God, hear me when I call to you; relieve my agony.
You are a true and righteous God; be merciful to me.

You fill my heart with greater joy than others get from wine.
Their harvest may be plentiful, but blessedness is mine!

I will lie down and sleep in peace; my rest is calm and sure.
I know that you alone, O God, can make my life secure.

From Psalm 4, put into verse by Bert Witvoet, 1984
(text modified by author)

Psalm 6

*(This might be the prayer of a
woman who was raped.)*

O God, do not rebuke me in anger or punish me in Your fury.
Have mercy on me, O God, for I am very weak.
Heal me, El Shaddai, for my bones ache with anguish,
and my soul is filled with turmoil.

O God, when will You deliver me from my despair?
For mercy's sake, come soon to me and save me!
If I die, how can I gratefully remember You?
If I stay in this dreadful pit, how can I praise You?

I am sick with sighing, and every night I soak my sheets with tears.
My face is wet with weeping, and my eyes are hollow with grief.
The attack on me has made me grow old. . . .

Depart from me, all you who would do me evil!
For God has heard the sound of my sorrow.
She has heard my pleas, and She accepts me as I am.
All who have hurt me shall know shame and trouble.
Dishonor will fall on their heads.

Psalm 61

*(This might be the prayer of a woman
cabinet member in government.)*

Hear my cry, El Shaddai, and listen to my prayer.
I have reached my limits, and my heart is faint.
O lead me to the high rock of Your safekeeping.
Be my protection in the midst of my foes.

Let me always abide in Your presence.
Hide me in the shelter of Your wings.

It comforts me that You, O God, have heard my solemn vows,
and have given me the heritage of all those who revere You.

I ask that You prolong the reign of good rulers and leaders.
May their kind endure for many generations!
May the upright be seated in authority before You, O God, forever.
Watch over them with faithful love.
Then I will sing Your praise and be able to keep my vows every day.

Reading: Luke 7:36-50 or selection from the Appendix

Prayer: Intercession for all the world's children and for a future of peace and plenty for them

Benediction: May God bless you and keep you.
May God make Her face shine on you and be gracious to you.
May God lift up the light of Her countenance upon you and give you peace. Amen.

Saturday

Praising God the Creator

MORNING PRAYER

Opening:

> This is the day our God has made!
> Let us be glad and rejoice in it!

Hymn Prayer:

> Holy God, while angels bless You, may a mortal sing Your Name?
> God of earth as well as angels, You are ev'ry creature's theme.
> God of ev'ry land and nation, Ancient of Eternal Days,
> sounded through the wide creation be Your just and endless praise.
>
> For the grandeur of Your nature, grand beyond a seraph's thought;
> for the wonders of creation, works with skill and kindness wrought;
> for Your providence that governs all that lives in Your domain,
> wings an angel, guides a sparrow: blessed be Your gentle reign.

Robert Robinson, 1774

Psalm 29

*(This might be the prayer of women artists
rejoicing in the beauty of creation.)*

O angels and all heavenly beings,
ascribe to God all glory and strength.
Let all creatures ascribe to El Shaddai the glory of Her name.
Let all people worship El Shaddai in the beauty of holiness.

Listen to the voice of God!
It sounds over the waters.
It thunders over the seas.
How powerful and majestic is Her voice!
It bends the mighty cedars.
It makes the hills skip like calves, and the mountains like a young wild ox.
The voice of God flashes fire!
The voice of God shakes the wilderness.
The voice of God makes the does give birth and makes the forests green.

In Her presence, all cry "Glory!"

El Shaddai rides on the waves.
El Shaddai reigns forever!

She will fill Her people with strength.
She will bless Her people with peace.

Psalm 136

(This might be the prayer of a woman rabbi leading her congregation.)

Let us give thanks to El Shaddai, for She alone is good.
Let us give thanks to the one true God, the One who rules over all.
Let us give thanks to the One who works wonders.
Her love endures forever!

With wisdom She made the heavens and set the lights in the sky.
She created the sun to rule the day, the moon and stars to rule the night.
She spread out the earth upon the waters.
Her love endures forever!

She struck down the pride of Egypt and rescued Her people from bondage.
With a strong hand and an outstretched arm She made a path in the sea.
She made Her people pass safely through its midst,
but drowned proud Pharaoh and all his hosts.
Her love endures forever!

She led Her people through the wilderness into the promised land.
She struck down kings and gave their land to Her poor and humble people.
She has always remembered us in our weakness and poverty.
She has rescued us over and over again from all who oppress us.
Her love endures forever!

It is She who gives food to all flesh, filling the earth with Her love.
O give thanks to the God of heaven!
Her love endures forever!

Reading: Job 38:1-11 or selection from the Appendix

Prayer: Intercession for all creation, the environment, all creatures, and the earth itself

Benediction: May God, who made darkness and light, day and night, watch over us and guide us in this new day to serve Her with gladness and joy. Amen.

MIDDAY PRAYER

Opening:

Our help is in the name of God,
who gave birth to the earth and the heavens.

Psalm 67
*(This might be the prayer of a woman delegate
at the United Nations.)*

May God's face shine upon us with mercy and blessing.
May Her ways be known in all the earth.
May all nations experience Her saving power and love.

Let all people everywhere praise El Shaddai!
Let all creatures of the earth honor God.
Let the nations be glad and sing for joy,
for She judges all people with justice,
and guides all who dwell in the earth.

The earth gives its harvest; its bounty is the blessing of God.
Let all the ends of the earth revere Her!
Let all people sing Her praise!

Silence

Prayer of the Faithful:

O God, grant us a deeper sense of fellowship with all living things,
our little brothers and sisters to whom, in common with us,
    You have given this earth as home.
We recall with regret that in the past we have acted high-handedly
    and cruelly
in exercising our domain over them.
Thus, the voice of the earth, which should have risen to you in song,
has turned into a groan of travail.
May we realize that all these creatures also live for themselves
    and for You —
not for us alone!
They too love the goodness of life, as we do,
and serve You better in their way than we do in ours.

St. Basil of Caesarea, 329-379

Benediction: May the love of God, the Creator of all; the beauty of Christ, the
        true Light of all; and the joy of the Holy Spirit, the true Life of all,
        fill our hearts and lives this day and always. Amen.

EVENING PRAYER

Opening:

Let our prayer rise before You like incense,
And the lifting up of our hands be an evening sacrifice.

Hymn Prayer:

We plow the fields and scatter the good seed on the land;
but it is fed and watered by God's almighty hand;
She sends the snow in winter, the warmth to swell the grain,
the breezes and the sunshine, and soft refreshing rain.

All good gifts around us are sent from heaven above;
then thank our God, O thank our God, for all Her love!

She only is the Maker of all things near and far;
She paints the wayside flower, She lights the evening star;
the winds and waves obey Her, by Her the birds are fed;
much more to us, Her children, She gives our daily bread.

All good gifts around us are sent from heaven above;
then thank our God, O thank our God, for all Her love!

We thank You, then, O Mother, for all things bright and good,
the seed-time and the harvest, our life, our health, our food;
accept the gifts we offer, for all Your love imparts;
and what You most desire, our humble, thankful hearts.

All good gifts around us are sent from heaven above;
then thank our God, O thank our God, for all Her love!

M. Claudius, 1782;
translated by Jane Montgomery-Campbell
in the nineteenth century
(text modified by author)

Psalm 8

(This might be the prayer of a woman astronomer.)

El Shaddai, how beautiful You are in all the earth!
Your glory shines in the heavens!
Little children give witness to Your greatness,
and Your adversary is silenced.

When I gaze in awe at the vast heavens You made,
the moon and the stars which are the work of Your fingers,
What are women that You are mindful of them,
or their daughters, that You visit them?

Yet You have made woman in Your image,
and crowned her with glory and honor!
You have given her dominion over the works of Your hands.
You have put all things in her keeping and care —
all sheep and cattle, and the wild beasts of the field and forest,
the birds of the air and the creatures of the sea.

El Shaddai, how beautiful is Your name in all the earth!

Psalm 139

(This might be the prayer of a pregnant woman.)

O God, You search me and know me inside out.
You know my comings and goings.
You understand my thoughts completely.
You examine my ways, whether waking or sleeping,
and are familiar with the habits of my being.
Before I speak a word, You already know it.
You are all around me, behind me and before me.
You lay Your loving hand on me, choosing me in love.
Such knowledge is too wonderful for me to comprehend.
It is utterly beyond me.

Where could I go to escape Your Spirit?
Where could I flee from Your presence?
Were I to go to the highest heavens, I would find You there.
Were I to descend into the depths of hell, even there I would find You!

Were I to take the red wings of dawn and flee to the sea's utmost end,
even there You would be leading me, and Your right hand would
    hold me fast!
Were I to say, "I will take cover in darkness," the night would turn to light.
For darkness is not dark to You.
The night shines like the day, and darkness is as bright as light.
Waking or sleeping, I am always with You.

You have formed my innermost parts.
You knit me together in the womb of my mother.
I thank You, for I am marvelously and wonderfully made!
All Your works are wonder-full, as my soul knows very well.
You clearly saw even my bones when You made me in secret,
when You wove me together in the dark depths of the womb.
Your eyes saw me as embryo, and before my days began, You shaped them.
My whole life is written in Your Book of Life!

How precious Your thoughts are to me, El Shaddai!
How great in number they are!
If I were to try and count them, it would be impossible,
like trying to count the grains of sand on the seashore.

Search me, O God, and examine my heart.
Try me, and test my motives and thoughts.
See if there be any evil in me,
and lead me in the way of eternal life.

Reading: Job 38:25-38 or selection from the Appendix

Prayer: Intercession for human creativity, the arts, all artists, and the flourishing of beauty in every part of society

Benediction: May God fill our hearts with peace and bless us with sleep that restores us for a new day. Amen.

Week Two

Sunday

Worshiping God Our Savior

MORNING PRAYER

Opening:

> In the morning, fill us with Your love,
> and we shall live this day in joy and praise!

Hymn Prayer:

> Christ, whose glory fills the skies, Christ, the true and only Light,
> Sun of Righteousness, arise, triumph o'er the shades of night;
> Dayspring from on high, be near; Daystar, in my heart appear.
>
> Dark and cheerless is the morn unaccompanied by thee;
> joyless is the day's return, till thy mercy's beams I see,
> till they inward light impart, till thou cheer and warm my heart.
>
> Visit then this soul of mine; pierce the gloom of sin and grief.
> Fill me, Radiancy Divine; scatter all my unbelief;
> more and more thyself display, shining to the Perfect Day.

Charles Wesley, 1739

Psalm 24

(This might be the processional prayer of women going to worship.)

The whole world and everything in it belong to El Shaddai.
All who dwell in it are Her possession.
It is She who made the dry land upon the seas,
who established the course of the rivers.

Who shall abide in Her holy presence?
Who shall stand in Her holy places?
Those who have clean hands and pure hearts;
those who are guileless and do not speak deceitfully;
those who seek the face of God.
They will be blessed by El Shaddai,
and vindicated by the God of Shalom.

O gates, lift yourselves up!
O doors, swing open!
Let the God of Glory enter!

Who is the God of Glory?
El Shaddai, strong and loving!
El Shaddai, mighty in mercy!

O gates, lift yourselves up!
O doors, swing open!
And the God of Glory will enter!

Who is the God of Glory?
El Shaddai, maker and leader of the hosts of heaven,
She is the God of Glory!

Psalm 43

(This might be the prayer of women who have been called by God to serve the church but have been refused ordination.)

O God, vindicate us!
Defend our cause against the hard-hearted!
Deliver us from defensive and unjust authorities!

O God, in You is our strength.
Will You ignore our plight?
Will You let us go on mourning because of their oppression?

Shed Your light and send out Your truth to lead us all.
Let them bring us to Your holy house — the sanctuary where You dwell.
Then we will go up to Your altar, O God.
With beautiful music we will offer eucharist to You,
        our Joy and our Delight!

O my soul, why are you so downcast?
Why do you groan within me?
Hope in El Shaddai!
For we women will someday offer eucharist to Her,
Who is our God and our Savior.

Reading: Judges 4:1-10 or selection from the Appendix

Prayer: Intercession for the local church

Benediction: May God, the Source of light, strength, and truth, bless us in this new day and week, and grant that we may walk in Her light, trust in Her strength, and be faithful to Her truth. Amen.

MIDDAY PRAYER

Opening:

O God, make speed to save us!
O Holy One, make haste to help us!

Psalm 26

*(This might be the prayer of a woman
protesting corruption in the church.)*

El Shaddai, justify me!
I have walked with integrity and trusted in You with constancy.
Purify my will and my heart.

I see Your many mercies, and I try to walk in the light of Your truth.
I do not make common cause with those who deceive,
nor do I participate in their dishonesty.
I have separated myself from the company of evildoers,
and I refuse to take part in their plans.
I wash my hands of their wrongdoing and proclaim my innocence.

I love to worship at Your altar, O God, singing a song of thanksgiving,
and praising Your wonderful works.
I love Your presence, El Shaddai, and the places where Your beauty shines!

Do not let me be swept along by evil,
caught up in the corruption of those who are far from You.
Preserve me from their forceful ways, their evil devices, their injustice.
For I choose to walk in integrity.
Graciously free me and firmly ground me.
Then I will bless You in the midst of upright congregations.

Psalm 99

(This might be the call to worship of faith-full women everywhere.)

El Shaddai reigns! Let the people who despise or ignore Her tremble!
She is carried on the wings of the cherubim.
Let the earth shudder with joy!
El Shaddai is magnified by Her people; let everyone exalt Her.
Let all peoples praise Her great and glorious name!
Holy is She!

God is a strong judge and a passionate lover of justice.
She has established equity as a basic rule of life.
She has always executed justice and acted uprightly toward all.
Exalt Her, therefore, and worship at Her feet, for holy is She!

She chose Miriam and Moses to serve Her.
Deborah and Samuel called on Her name.
When they cried to El Shaddai, She answered them.
She spoke to them in the cloud of Her glory.
They, in turn, treasured Her testimonies,
and taught others the statutes She gave them.
God answered them, forgave them, and avenged all wrong against them.

Exalt El Shaddai our God, and worship in Her holy presence.
For She alone is holy!

Silence

Prayer of the Faithful:

We beg you, O God, be our help and strength.
Save those among us who are oppressed, have pity on the lowly,
    and lift up the fallen.
Heal the sick, bring back the straying, and feed the hungry.
Release those in prison, steady those who falter,
    and strengthen the faint-hearted.
Let all nations come to know You, the one True God,
    and Your Son Jesus Christ,
and us Your people and the sheep of Your pasture.

Do not keep count of the sins of Your servants,
but purify us through the bath of Your truth,
and direct our steps.
Help us to walk in holiness of heart,
and to do what is good and pleasing in Your eyes.
Let Your face shine on us to grant us every good in peace,
to protect us by Your powerful hand,
to deliver us from every evil by the might of Your arm,
and to save us from the unjust hatred of our adversaries.
Grant to us and to all who dwell on this earth peace and harmony, O God.

St. Clement I, 38-101

Benediction: May God, the Lover of justice, the Savior of the poor,
and the Keeper of all the earth
bless us this day and throughout our lives. Amen.

EVENING PRAYER

Opening:

Let Your servants now rest in peace, O God,
for our eyes have seen Your salvation.

Hymn Prayer:

Savior, again to Thy dear name we raise
with one accord our evening hymn of praise;
Guard Thou our lips from sin, our hearts from shame,
that in this day have called upon Thy name.

Grant us Thy peace, God, through the coming night;
turn Thou for us its darkness into light;
from harm and danger keep Thy children free,
for dark and light are both alike to Thee.

Grant us Thy peace throughout our earthly life;
peace to Thy church from error and from strife;
peace to our land, the fruit of truth and love;
peace in each heart, Thy Spirit from above.

Thy peace in life, the balm of ev'ry pain;
Thy peace in death, the hope to rise again;
then when Thy voice shall bid our conflict cease,
call us, O God, to Thy eternal peace.

John Ellerton, 1866
(text modified by author)

Psalm 138

(This might be the prayer of a woman priest.)

With my whole heart I thank You, El Shaddai!
Before all the powers of heaven and earth I sing Your praise.
I worship in Your sanctuary, offering eucharist in Your name.
Your name and Your Word proclaim Your love and faithfulness.
When I call upon You, You answer me.
You have made me bold and given strength to my soul.

I call upon all the rulers of earth to offer You praise, El Shaddai!
I proclaim the words of Your mouth, that all may know Your will.

Let all people praise the ways of God and the greatness of Her glory!
For though Her reign extends over all, She stoops to care for the lowly.
But She keeps Her distance from the proud and arrogant.

When I walk in the midst of trouble, She watches over me.
When my adversaries rise up against me,
She stretches out Her hand and delivers me.
She fulfills Her purpose for me.

O God, Your mercy endures forever!
I know that You will never forsake the work of Your hands.

Psalm 27

(This might be the prayer of young women protesting injustice.)

Since God is our light and our salvation, we need not fear anyone!
Since She is the strength of our life, we can act with courage.
When unjust people attack us, and others devour us with slander,
they will stumble and fall.
Though an army encamp against us, our hearts will be unafraid.
Though violence be threatened against us, we will remain confident.

We ask this one thing of God —
that we may abide in Her presence
    all the days of our lives.
We seek above all to behold Her beauty,
and to study the wisdom of Her ways.

She will hide us in Her secret shelter in times of trouble.
She will offer us sanctuary in the hidden places of Her holiness.
She will set us solidly upon the rock of Her purposes,
so that we cannot be shaken.
We will always be filled with the joy of Her presence,
and sing praises to El Shaddai!

God hears us when we call to Her and answers us with great favor.
She bids us seek Her face.

We will indeed seek Her face, trusting that She will not turn away,
will not withdraw from us in anger.
She has always been our help.
She will not leave us now or forsake us.
When even our mothers and fathers withdraw their love and support,
God will gather us in Her loving arms.

Teach us Your ways, O God, and make Your paths plain to us.
In the face of the scrutiny of those who are hostile,
do not let us give in to fear or yield to dread.
Many speak out with lies against us, threatening violence and harm.
But we believe that we shall see Your goodness as long as we live!

O sisters, wait with us for El Shaddai!
Be strong, and let your hearts take courage.
Yes — wait confidently for God!

Reading: Judges 5:1-15 and 19-21 or selection from the Appendix

Prayer: Intercession for the worldwide church, especially for its unity

Benediction: May the God who shelters us in trouble, makes our path plain, and showers us with goodness grant us the blessing of Her constant presence and give us the constant awareness of it. Amen.

Monday

Hoping in God Our Future

MORNING PRAYER

Opening:

In the morning, fill us with Your love,
and we shall live this day in joy and praise!

Hymn Prayer:

Morning glory, starlit sky, soaring music, scholars' truth,
flight of swallows, autumn leaves, memory's treasure, grace of youth:
open are the gifts of God, gifts of love to mind and sense;
hidden is love's agony, love's endeavor, love's expense.

Love that gives, gives evermore, gives with zeal, with eager hands;
spares not, keeps not, all outpours, ventures all, its all expends.
Drained is love in making full, bound in setting others free,
poor in making many rich, weak in giving power to be.

Therefore Christ who shows us God helpless hangs upon the tree,
and the nails and crown of thorns tell of what God's love must be.
Here is God: no monarch he, throned in easy state to reign;
here is God, whose arms of love, aching, spent, the world sustain.

W. H. Vanstone, 1980

Psalm 33

(This might be the prayer of a woman environmentalist.)

It is fitting for the upright to praise El Shaddai with dances of joy!
Let us sing a new song of thanksgiving to Her with stringed instruments!
Let us sing aloud of Her glory with sweet and skillful playing!

For God's Word is trustworthy, and Her works are faithful.
She loves what is right and just.
The whole world is full of Her steadfast love.

By El Shaddai's word the heavens came into being.
Her creative spirit still brings forth stars and galaxies.
She gathered the waters together and heaped them into seas.
She set storehouses of treasures in their hidden depths.

Let all the earth revere El Shaddai!
Let all who dwell upon earth live in awe of Her.
For She spoke, and all came to be.
She is the Mother of the universe!

God voids the counsel of the nations and frustrates their plans.
Leaders are not saved by military might.
Soldiers are not delivered by superior weapons.
The best armaments are a vain hope for peace.
The greatest human skill cannot establish Shalom.
But God's counsel stands forever, and Her word guides each generation.

Blessed are the people who honor El Shaddai as God.
She chooses them as Her heritage.
From heaven She surveys all creatures.
She who shapes our hearts knows our thoughts and deeds.
Look! The eye of El Shaddai rests on those who revere Her.
Those who hope in Her steadfast love are delivered from inner death;
their souls do not starve, even in famine.

Wait, then, for God, who is our help and our protection.
Let your heart rejoice in Her, and trust in Her holy name.

Psalm 108
*(This might be the prayer of a woman
diplomat at the United Nations.)*

With my heart fixed on You, O God, I will make glorious melody!
I will take up musical instruments and with singing awake the dawn!
I will thank You, El Shaddai, among all the peoples.
I will praise You among all the representatives of the nations.
For Your mercy is as high as the sky,
and Your faithfulness reaches to the clouds.
Be exalted above the heavens, O God,
    and let Your glory fill the whole earth!
Deliver Your beloved ones, and save me with Your hand of love.
Answer my prayer!

God speaks in Her holiness:
"I rejoice in the cultures of the earth's varied peoples.
I grant them the land they live on.
I claim many peoples as mine, to use for my saving purposes.
I will shout in triumph over those who fight against me and my will."

Think about this: who can help us reach our goals if God rejects us?
She does not march forth with our armies.
Human help is vain if God's grace is absent from our struggles.
But with God, we can do great things.
It is She who will defeat all violence.

Reading: 1 Samuel 2:1-10 or selection from the Appendix

Prayer: Intercession for the immediate family

Benediction: May the God of great mercy and faithfulness fill our lives with Her
glory and praise, and speedily accomplish Her saving purposes for
us and all people. Amen.

MIDDAY PRAYER

Opening:

O God, make speed to save us!
O Holy One, make haste to help us!

Psalm 18:1-19
*(This might be the prayer of a woman delivered
from her desire to commit suicide.)*

I love You, El Shaddai, my strength!
You are my rock, my shelter, and my Savior.

My God is a rock to me, and in Her I find the refuge I need.
I cling to Her to be saved, and She delivers me and makes me whole!
She is like a high wall behind which I can hide from destruction.
When I call on Her and offer Her praise, I am saved from my inner foes.

I felt the cords of death hemming me in and the waves
    of destruction washing over me.
Deadly chains of despair encircled me, and I faced the end of my life.
I cried to God in my distress; I begged El Shaddai to help me.

She heard my cry!

The ground of my despair shook and trembled.
The foundations of my mountains of trouble moved, mightily shaken!
The smoke and fire of God's hot anger burned against my foes.
She came down from heaven and put the darkness within me under Her feet.
She flew to my rescue on the wings of the angels.
She soared on the wings of the wind, robing Herself with my darkness.
The dark clouds in my soul became Her pavilion.
Brightness like lightning surrounded Her,
    piercing the heavy gloom within me.
Her heavenly thunder and flashing lightning scattered my foes within!
I saw the life-giving rivers of water that flowed within me.
She laid bare the foundations of my despair,
and rebuked the turmoil raging within me.

Then She reached from on high and took me,
    drawing me out of the flood of despair.
She delivered me from my strong enemy, from the self-hatred within.

My inner foes were too much for me.
When I confronted them, I faced calamity.
But El Shaddai was my support.
She brought me into a safe and comforting place.
She took delight in delivering me!

Therefore I will keep El Shaddai's ways and never depart from Her.

Psalm 133

(This might be the prayer of women's worshiping communities.)

Look how good and pleasant it is when sisters live together in unity!
It is like precious oil upon the head that runs down the hair,
down the long locks of a priest or prophet,
    down onto the collar of her robes!
It is like the dew of the holy presence,
which falls where God's people gather.
There God has commanded Her blessing — life forevermore!

Silence

Prayer of the Faithful

El Shaddai, You are the earth beneath our feet,
the ground of our being,
and the Womb of all.
You birth the earth,
groaning with great labor pain in all our suffering and dying.
Your golden joys and scarlet sorrows
fall onto death's dark soil,
and nourish the grain that becomes the Bread of Life.
We harvest Your bounty,
we feast on Your beauty,
and are nourished and comforted at the breasts of Your goodness.

Anonymous, 20th century

Benediction: May the God who is our Hope in calamity, our Rescuer in trouble, and our Protection from the assaults of evil bless and keep us through this day and throughout our lives. Amen.

EVENING PRAYER

Opening:

Let Your servants now rest in peace, O God,
for our eyes have seen Your salvation.

Hymn Prayer:

If you but trust in God to guide you, and place your confidence in Her,
you'll find Her always there beside you to give you hope and
     strength within;
for those who trust God's changeless love build on the rock
     that will not move.

Only be still, and wait Her pleasure in cheerful hope with heart content.
She fills your needs to fullest measure with what discerning Love has sent;
doubt not our inmost wants are known to Her who chose us for Her own.

Georg Neumark, 1657
(text modified by author)

Psalm 18:25-36, 49
(This might be the prayer of a woman working for social justice.)

The merciful can see Your mercy.
The just can see Your justice.
The pure can see Your purity.
But You appear perverse to those who are evil.

You save afflicted people, but You bring down the high and mighty.
El Shaddai, You light my lamp and make my darkness bright!
With Your help I can escape from my enemies.
With You I can leap over any wall!

El Shaddai is perfect in Her ways, and all Her promises prove true.
Who is our Rock, save God? She protects all who take refuge in Her.
El Shaddai girds me with strength and makes my way secure.
She sets my feet securely on the heights, as if I were a deer.
She teaches me how to bear conflict and how to bend what is strong.
She shields me with salvation, and Her right hand holds me up.
Her gentleness has made me strong!
She has made a wide place for my steps, so that I do not slip.

For this I will praise You among the nations, El Shaddai.
I will sing glad songs to glorify Your name!

Psalm 134

Come, bless El Shaddai, all you friends of God,
     you who stand tonight in Her presence.
Lift up your hands in this holy place,
and bless El Shaddai through the night.
May God bless you from Her holy dwelling,
She who births both heaven and earth!

Reading: Luke 1:46-56 or selection from the Appendix

Prayer: Intercession for the extended family

Benediction: May the God of gentleness, support, and sustaining love gather us
in Her arms this night and bless us with sleep that restores both body
and soul. Amen.

Tuesday

Seeking God's Wisdom

MORNING PRAYER

Opening:

In the morning, fill us with Your love,
and we shall live this day in joy and praise!

Hymn Prayer:

In sweet communion, God, with You I constantly abide;
my hand You hold within Your own to keep me near Your side.

Your Wisdom through my earthly way shall guide me, and control,
and then to glory afterward You will receive my soul.

Whom have I, God, in heaven but You, to whom my thoughts aspire?
And having You, on earth is nought that I can yet desire.

Though flesh and heart should faint and fail, my God will ever be
the strength and portion of my heart, my Joy eternally.

To live apart from God is death; 'tis good Her face to seek;
my refuge is the living God; Her praise I long to speak.

Psalm 73, appearing in verse form in *The Psalter*, 1912
(text modified by author)

Psalm 19
(This might be the prayer of a woman teacher.)

The spacious heavens declare the glorious handiwork of God.
Day and night speak out, although no words are heard.
They sound their proclamation without the use of speech.
Their divine direction reaches to the ends of the earth;
their message fills the whole world.

God has made the sky a tent for the sun.
It rises in the canopy above with the gladness of a bridegroom.
It runs its course through the sky with the strength of an athlete.
The orbit of the sun extends from one end of heaven to the other.
Nothing can hide from its heat.

The soul is restored by the Word of God.
The simple are made wise by Her sure testimony.
The heart is made joyful by Her just judgments.
The eyes are enlightened by Her clear commands.

The purposes of God are pure; they stand, unstained, forever.
The precepts of God are faithful, fair, and right.
They are more desirable than much fine gold,
    sweeter than drops of amber honey.
They provide needed warning to God's children,
and there is great reward in keeping them.

O God, who among us can discern our hidden sinfulness?
Acquit us of our secret faults!
Keep Your children from committing arrogant sins.
Do not let pride or prejudice get the upper hand.
Then we shall be whole, and innocent of serious transgression.

Let the words of our mouths and the meditations of our hearts
find favor with You, our Rock and our Redeemer!

Psalm 111
(This might be the prayer of a woman elder.)

> Alleluia! I am eager to thank God wholeheartedly,
> to praise Her in the council of the upright, in the midst of the congregation.
>
> Great are God's works, and all who delight in them study them.
> All She does is honorable and glorious, and Her righteousness lasts forever!
> She performs wonderful deeds of mercy and grace,
>   and we cherish their memory.
> She feeds the souls of Her children and keeps covenant with them forever.
> She shows Her people the power of Her salvation,
>   and bestows on them a rich heritage.
> All the works of Her hands are faithful and just.
> All Her precepts, established forever, are trustworthy.
> Truth and righteousness lie in following them.
> El Shaddai frees Her people and creates an eternal covenant with them.
>
> Holy and awesome is Her name!
> To revere Her is to begin to be wise.
> To practice Her presence is to grow in understanding.
> Her praise will endure forever!

Reading: Luke 8:1-3 or selection from the Appendix

Prayer: Intercession for friends and neighbors

Benediction: May the Holy Spirit of Wisdom,
        whose truth and faithfulness guide and keep us,
        fill this day with Her blessing. Amen.

MIDDAY PRAYER

Opening:

> O God, make speed to save us!
> O Holy One, make haste to help us!

*(This might be the prayer of a woman executive
in a multinational corporation.)*

Blessed are all who walk uprightly in the ways of El Shaddai.
Blessed are all who keep Her commands and wholeheartedly seek Her will.
Blessed are those who avoid wrongdoing and follow Her paths of justice.

O God, You have asked us to keep Your precepts with great care.
May I be steadfast in yielding to Your guidance!
As long as I fix my eyes on Your will, I will never be put to shame.
When I learn Your righteous ways, I will have integrity of heart.
With gratitude I will keep Your commands.
I know You will not forsake me.

How shall I purify my path?
By living according to Your Word!
I have sought You with my whole heart —
do not let me wander away.
I have hid Your Word in my heart,
for it keeps me from sinning against You.

Blessed El Shaddai, teach me the wisdom of Your way.
With my lips I shall declare all Your ordinances.
I take more pleasure in Your instruction than in plentiful power and riches.
I will meditate on Your guidelines and fix my gaze on Your ways.
I will delight myself in Your promises.
I will never forget Your Word.

In Your mercy help me to live Your Word.
Open my eyes to see the marvels of Your precepts.
I am a traveler in need of direction;
do not hide Your wisdom from me.
My soul is filled with longing for what You have commanded.

The proud who wander from Your will are cursed with Your rebuke.
Remove the reproach and scorn they heap on me
        when I try to obey Your law.
When the powerful sit plotting against me, I will meditate on Your Word.
Your precepts are my delight; Your commands are my counselors.

When my soul lies in the dust, restore me with Your Word of life.
When I entreat You, teach my heart Your ways.
When my soul sinks with grief, strengthen me with Your wisdom.
Save me from lying ways, and enlighten me with Your favor.
I choose to follow the way of truth and faithfulness.
I hold Your judgments steadily before me.
I cling to Your Word, El Shaddai.
Do not let me be put to shame.
I will run in the way of Your wisdom as You enlarge my heart.

Silence

Prayer of the Faithful

O eternal Word of my God,
I want to spend my life in heeding You.
I want to be wholly teachable so that I may learn everything from You.
Then throughout all the nights, all the emptinesses, all the powerlessnesses,
I want to concentrate on You alone and dwell beneath Your great light. . . .

O consuming Fire, Spirit of love, inundate me
so that my soul will become like an incarnation of the Word. . . .

And You, O Creator, bend down toward Your creature.
See in her only Your Beloved in whom You have placed
all Your good pleasure.

O my Threesome, my All and my Blessing, infinite Solitude,
and Immensity in Whom I lose myself,
I give myself to You as a prize.
Bury Yourself in me so that I may bury myself in You,
while waiting to contemplate in Your light the abyss of Your greatness.

Elizabeth of the Trinity, 1880-1900

Benediction: May the eternal Word of God bless our lives this day and always
with steadfast faithfulness to Her will and ways. Amen.

EVENING PRAYER

Opening:

Let Your servants now rest in peace, O God,
for our eyes have seen Your salvation.

Hymn Prayer:

How blest is she who fearing God, from sin restrains her feet;
who will not with the wicked stand, who shuns the scorner's seat.

How blest is she who makes God's law her treasure and delight,
and meditates upon Her Word with gladness day and night.

Her life is nourished like a tree set by the river's side —
its leaf is green, its fruit is sure; so all her works abide.

> Psalm 1, appearing in this verse form in *The Psalter,* 1912
> (text modified by author)

Psalm 119:33-56
(This might be the prayer of a woman attorney.)

Teach me Your laws, O God, and I will keep them to the end.
Help me to understand Your commands and follow them wholeheartedly.
Make me walk in the way of Your will, for in it I take great delight!
Incline my heart to Your wisdom rather than to unjust gain.
Avert my eyes from empty show and give me life in Your way.
Make Your Word sure to me, for I am devoted to You.
Turn away the reproach which I dread.
Let all see that Your judgments are just and good.

How I long for Your wisdom!
In Your generosity, give me life.
In Your mercy, make me whole, according to Your promise.
Grant me an answer for those who taunt me because I trust in You.
Let me always speak truthfully and rely on You for justice.

I promise to keep Your law now and as long as You give me life.
I know that when I follow Your will, I will walk in freedom!

I will speak of Your justice to the powerful and will not be ashamed.
I will delight myself in what You desire and love what You command.
I will devote myself to Your law and lovingly muse on Your will.

Remember Your promise to me, on which my hopes rest.
When I am afflicted, Your Word gives me life.
Although the godless deride me, I will not turn from Your law.
When I remember Your judgments, I find the comfort I need.

When I see how the wicked forsake Your law, I am seized with horror.
But Your wisdom has been my joy and my song,
   my faithful companion throughout my earthly pilgrimage.
In the night I remember Your name, El Shaddai,
and I dearly treasure Your will.
What a blessing it is to me that I have kept Your commands!

Reading: Mark 3:31-35 or selection from the Appendix

Prayer: Intercession for enemies/adversaries/competitors

Benediction: May the God whose will is our portion and delight
bless us with the wisdom to walk and rest in that will day and night!
Amen.

Wednesday

Trusting in God Our Refuge

MORNING PRAYER

Opening:

In the morning, fill us with Your love,
and we shall live this day in joy and praise!

Hymn Prayer:

New ev'ry morning is the love our waking and uprising prove;
through sleep and darkness safely brought, restored to life,
    and pow'r, and thought.

New mercies each returning day hover around us while we pray;
new perils past, new sins forgiv'n, new thoughts of God,
    new hopes of heav'n.

If on our daily course our mind be set to hallow all we find,
new treasures still of countless price God will provide for sacrifice.

The trivial work, the common task will furnish all we need or ask
of many ways in this new day to live more nearly as we pray.

John Keble, 1827

Psalm 28
(This might be the prayer of a woman
community organizer among the poor.)

When I call to You, O God my Rock, do not be deaf to my pleas!
If You do not respond to me, I will fall into deadly despair.
Hear me as I cry for help with my arms stretched out to You.
Deliver me from the deceit of the wicked.
They speak peace to their neighbors, but destruction is in their hearts.
Give them what their deeds deserve, a fitting return for their evil.
Turn the work of their hands against them, and do to them
     as they have done.
When they ignore Your will and scorn the work of Your hands,
break them down and let them never be built up again.

Blessed be El Shaddai, for She has heard my prayers!
She is my strength, a strong wall of protection.
My heart trusted in Her, and She helped me.
Therefore my heart dances for joy as I sing songs of thanksgiving.
El Shaddai is the strength of all Her children,
     the refuge of Her chosen ones.
She saves Her people and blesses Her heritage.
She nourishes them and upholds them forever!

Psalm 123
(This might be the prayer of women in
any land who have been put down.)

To You, O God, we lift up our eyes, seeking Your heavenly help.
As the eyes of workers look to a generous employer,
and as the eyes of children look to a kind mother,
so our eyes look to You, El Shaddai, seeking Your mercy on us.

Show us Your compassion, O God, for You know
     how we have been scorned.
For too long our souls have been bruised by contempt,
the disdain of those who lord it over us, at ease in their "superior" place.

Reading: Luke 10:38-41 or selection from the Appendix

Prayer: Intercession for the community/town/city

Benediction: May God, who is utterly trustworthy, bless us with growing confidence in Her love and Her promises, that we may walk this day, and every day, in close communion with Her. Amen.

MIDDAY PRAYER

Opening:

> O God, make speed to save us!
> O Holy One, make haste to help us!

Psalm 52
(This might be the prayer of exploited
women migrant workers.)

> O mighty men, why do you do evil, in spite of God's steadfast love?
> Your tongues pierce like razors, deceitfully cutting our hopes.
> You love evil more than good, lying more than speaking uprightly.
> You love words and deeds that devour, and your mouths are filled with lies.
>
> Be sure that God will pluck you from your place of power.
> She will break down your injustice completely.
> She will uproot you from the land of the living.
>
> When we the oppressed see this, we will no longer fear you.
> We will revere God and laughingly say,
> "See the men who would not honor God, but trusted in their riches,
> and thought their power was secure!"

As for us, we will be like olive trees, greening in the presence of God!
We will trust in Her steadfast love every day — indeed, forever.
We will offer Her thanks as long as we live for all that She has done.
We will wait for Her and proclaim Her goodness
    in the company of the godly.

Silence

Prayer of the Faithful:

Slow me down, God.
Ease the pounding of my heart by the quieting of my mind.
Steady my hurried pace with a vision of the eternal reach of time.
Give me, amid the confusion of the day, the calmness of the everlasting hills.
Break the tensions of my nerves and muscles with the soothing music
of the singing streams that live in my memory.
Help me to know the magical, restoring power of sleep.
Teach me the art of taking minute vacations —
of slowing down to look at a flower, to chat with a friend, to pat a dog,
    to read a few lines from a good book.
Remind me each day of the fable of the hare and the tortoise,
that I may know that the race is not always to the swift —
that there is more to life than increasing its speed.
Let me look upward into the branches of the towering oak
and know that it grew great and strong because it grew slowly and well.
Slow me down, God, and inspire me to send my roots deep
into the soil of life's enduring values,
that I may grow toward the stars of my greater destiny.

Richard Cushing, 1895-1970

Benediction: May the God of all blessing grant us the grace to be like fruitful trees, greening in the house of Her presence, rooted in Her life-giving water, and bearing fruit for Her glory, today and always. Amen.

EVENING PRAYER

Opening:

Let Your servants now rest in peace, O God,
for our eyes have seen Your salvation.

Hymn Prayer:

Abide with me; fast falls the eventide;
the darkness deepens; God, with me abide!
When other helpers fail and comforts flee,
Help of the helpless, O abide with me.

Swift to its close ebbs out life's little day;
earth's joys grow dim, its glories pass away;
change and decay in all around I see;
O Thou who changest not, abide with me!

I need Thy presence every passing hour;
what but Thy grace can foil the tempter's power?
Who like Thyself my guide and stay can be?
Through cloud and sunshine, O abide with me!

I fear no foe, with Thee at hand to bless;
ills have no weight, and tears no bitterness.
Where is death's sting? Where, grave, thy victory?
I triumph still, if Thou abide with me.

H. F. Lyte, 1847

Psalm 36
*(This might be the confession of a woman
struggling against envy and greed.)*

Within my heart, the shadow of transgression speaks wickedly;
there is no reverence for God in its eyes.
It flatters itself that its folly cannot be found out.
The words of its mouth are harmful and deceitful;

81

it leads me away from acting wisely and well.
It plots mischief during the night; it is up to no good; it does not spurn evil.

But Your steadfast love, El Shaddai, stretches as high as the sky.
Your faithfulness is as firm as the earth.
Your justice is as lasting as the mountains.
Your judgments are as deep as the sea.
You deliver all creatures, O God.

How precious is Your steadfast love, El Shaddai!
The children of earth take refuge in the shadow of Your wings.
You let them feast on Your abundance;
You let them drink from waterfalls of delight.
For You are the Fountain of Life!
And in Your light we are able to see light!
Continue to show Your lovingkindness to all who know You,
Your generosity to all the upright of heart.

Let me be unmoved by the shadow of evil that hides in my soul.
Defeat the evil within me. Thrust it down so it cannot rise up.

Psalm 146
*(This might be the prayerful advice of
a woman judge ready to retire.)*

Alleluia! Praise El Shaddai, O my soul!
I will praise El Shaddai as long as I live;
I will sing praises to God forever!

Do not trust in powerful people, for they are only human;
they have no salvation to offer.
One day they will breathe their last and return to the earth;
in that day their proud plans will perish.

Blessed are you who go to the God of our foremothers for help,
who trust in El Shaddai, the God who gave birth to heaven and earth,
the seas and all that is in them.
She is faithful to us forever!
She executes justice for the oppressed.

She gives food to the hungry.
She sets the prisoners free.
She opens the eyes of the blind.
She raises the disheartened and disabled.
She loves the just and generous.
She preserves the vulnerable stranger.
She sustains women and children,
those who have no one who will help them.
But She frustrates the ways of the wicked.

El Shaddai will reign forever!
Our God, O holy people, will be with us through all generations.
Alleluia!

Reading: Matthew 18:1-6 or selection from the Appendix

Prayer: Intercession for the larger community/state/province

Benediction: May the God who frees the captive, saves the oppressed, and relieves the poor bless us with the grace to act in solidarity with Her on their behalf. Amen!

Thursday

Crying Out to God for Justice and Mercy

MORNING PRAYER

Opening:

In the morning, fill us with Your love,
and we shall live this day in joy and praise!

Hymn Prayer:

Hear, O God, my urgent prayer as I come to seek Your care.
With each morning light I raise voice and heart in prayer and praise.

You do not delight in sin, or in tales that liars spin.
Haughty ones You will defeat, with all those who love deceit.

By Your mercy and Your grace, I will come before Your face.
Fearing foes, I bow to pray: lead me, God, make straight my way.

From Psalm 5, put into verse by Marie J. Post, 1983

Psalm 31
(This might be the prayer of an addicted woman.)

I seek refuge in You, El Shaddai, to save me from my shame.
In Your generosity, listen to me and quickly come to my help!
Be my strong rock, my place of protection!
For Your name's sake, lead me and guide me.
Release me from the net in which I am caught.
Because You alone can heal and make me whole,
into Your hands I commit my soul and spirit.
I trust Your faithful love to redeem me and set me free.

I will separate myself from those who follow false values.
I will reject all the false gods that society worships.
I will put my constant trust in no one else but You, El Shaddai.

Whenever I remember Your compassion, my heart is filled with joy.
I know You see my affliction and understand all that troubles me.
You will not abandon me to that which would harm me.
You will set me in a safe and spacious place.

Let me experience Your grace, O God, for I am in deep trouble.
My eyes ache with grief, and my body and soul waste away.
My life is spent in sorrow; my days are filled with sighs.
Because of sin, both my own and others', I grow weak and old.
Even my bones feel brittle with age.
I am scorned by my foes and avoided by my neighbors.
My acquaintances dread meeting me;
        those who see me in the street turn away.
I feel as forgotten as the dead whose memory no longer comes to mind.
I feel like a broken clay pot, my whole life shattered and broken.
The slander of many comes to my ears.
I am afraid of those whose plots might destroy my life.

But I will trust in You, El Shaddai. You alone are my God.
My life and times are in Your hands.
Save me from those who are against me,
who persecute me without cause.
In Your mercy rescue me, and let Your face shine on me with love.
O God, let me not be confounded for having called upon You.

Rather, confound the wicked, and let them go, struck dumb, to hell!
Silence lips that lie, that speak scornfully with reckless pride.

How great is the goodness You have stored up for those devoted to You!
You work on behalf of those who trust You in ways that all can see.
Your sheltering presence protects them from all attacks.
Blessed are You for working all these wonders!
When I was besieged and beset, You showed me steadfast love.
Though I said in my impatience, "You don't even see me!"
You heard my pleas when I cried for Your help.

Love El Shaddai, all you Her saints!
She preserves the faithful but brings down the high and mighty.
Have courage, all you who hope in Her, and She will strengthen your hearts.

Psalm 143

(This might be the prayer of a woman in deep depression.)

O God, hear my prayer, and listen to my pleading.
Answer me in Your faithfulness.
Be generous to me and do not condemn me,
remembering that before You, no one is sinless.

You know how the Adversary has pursued my soul,
how the Enemy crushes the vitality within me.
I am dwelling in deathly darkness, as if I had died long ago.
My spirit is faint within me, and my heart is stunned with despair.

I try to remember Your saving deeds from the past.
I muse upon Your handiwork.
I stretch out my hands to You.
But my soul is like a dry and weary land.

Hurry to help me, El Shaddai! My spirit is sinking fast!
Do not hide Your face from me, lest I fall into the pit of despair.
Let me hear words of love every morning, for I place my trust in You.
Show me the path I should take, for I commit my soul to You.
Deliver me from my enemies within, for I hide myself in Your grace.
Since You alone are my God, teach me to do Your will.

Lead me by Your Holy Spirit into a warm and heartening place.
For Your name's sake, El Shaddai, let my spirit live!
In Your mercy, save my soul and cut off my inner enemies.
In Your compassion, destroy what afflicts me within!
For I am Your child, and I trust You.

Reading: Mark 5:21-34 or selection from the Appendix

Prayer: Intercession for one's own country

Benediction: May the God of mercy, kindness, and steadfast love bless us with Her saving power in all the struggles of our life. Amen.

MIDDAY PRAYER

Opening:

O God, make speed to save us!
O Holy One, make haste to help us!

Psalm 10
(This might be the prayer of a woman
in a gang-infested neighborhood.)

O God, You seem so far away!
You seem to be in hiding in these times of trouble.
In pride the wicked pursue the poor, trapping them in violent schemes.
Evildoers indulge their hearts' wicked desires,
and the greedy despise God's just will.
"There is no God," they say to themselves.

Their ways seem to be prospering.
They do not see or grasp Your judgments.
They think that they are untouchable, that calamity will never strike them.
Their mouths are filled with cursing, their hearts with deceit and hate.
Their tongues are filled with mischief and fraud.

They sit in deserted doorways and alleys,
poised to ambush and murder the innocent.
Their eyes keep a sharp lookout for the helpless.
They lurk under cover like beasts, lying in wait for the weak.
So many of us stumble and are crushed by their violent strength.
These wicked men think God overlooks them, does not see their crimes.

O God, rouse Yourself and lift Your hand to save us!
Do not forget us in our affliction!
Do not let the wicked get away with renouncing You.
Do not let them say in their hearts, "God will never call us to account."
You certainly see the trouble they cause.
Repay them with Your righteous hand, we pray.

The helpless commit themselves to Your care,
for You are the Guardian of abandoned little ones.

Break the power of these worshipers of violence.
Search out and destroy all their evil.
For You, El Shaddai, will reign forever,
but the wicked shall perish from the earth.

O God, You hear the cry of the humble and fix their hearts firmly on You.
You give fair hearing and just judgment to children and all the oppressed,
so that cruelty might be restrained, and the violent terrorize no more.

Psalm 142

*(This might be the prayer of a woman
in desperate financial straits.)*

I cry to El Shaddai in fear.
I call to God in prayer.
I pour out my thoughts before Her,
telling Her all my troubles.
When my spirit is faint, She upholds me.

But a trap lies waiting in the path I walk.
There is no one who befriends me.
No one offers a way out;
no one cares about my dilemma.

I cry to El Shaddai, saying,
"I have no hope or refuge except in You."

She will attend to my cry when I am laid low.
She will deliver me from my pursuers, who are so much stronger than I.
She will rescue me from my desperate plight, and I will offer Her thanks!
She will surround me with generous people and reward me with goodness.

Silence

Prayer of the Faithful:

O God, You are the ineffable Ocean of Love,
the unfathomable Abyss of Peace,
the Source of all goodness, and the Dispenser of affection.
You send peace to those who are receptive to it.
Open for us today the sea of Your love,
and water us with the plentiful streams
from the riches of Your grace.

Make us children of tranquility and heirs of peace.
Enkindle in us the flame of Your love, and sow in us reverence for You.
Firm up our weakness by Your strength, and unite us closely
with You and with one another
in a bond of indissoluble unity and firm accord.

Syrian Clementine liturgy

Benediction: May God our Deliverer bring us out of whatever bondage we suffer,
and bless us with receptive hearts and open hands
to receive all that She longs to give. Amen.

EVENING PRAYER

Opening:

Let Your servants now rest in peace, O God,
for our eyes have seen Your salvation.

Hymn Prayer:

O God of earth and altar, in mercy hear our cry;
our earthly rulers falter, our people drift and die;
the walls of gold entomb us, the words of scorn divide;
take not Thy thunder from us, but take away our pride.

From all that terror teaches, from lies of pen and tongue;
from all the easy speeches that satisfy the throng;
from sale and profanation of honor and the word;
from sleep and from damnation, deliver us, good God!

G. K. Chesterton, 1906

Psalm 35
*(This might be the prayer of women who have been sexually
abused by fathers or husbands or other men close to them.)*

O God, confront those who abuse us!
Fight against those who attack us!
Rise up to help and defend us!
Use Your might against those who violate us!
Deliver our bodies and souls from those who are ruining our lives!
Shame and disgrace them, frustrate and confound them!
Let the wind of Your wrath drive them away like chaff.
Chase them into ways that are slippery and dark.
For without cause they trap us and hold us down.
Let retribution take them unawares.
Let the net of violence which they try to conceal snare them,
enmesh them in their own destructiveness.

Then we will rejoice in You and praise You for Your deliverance.
Then we will say,
"Who is a God like El Shaddai?
She delivers vulnerable women from men who overpower them.
She saves children from those who violate them."

They attack us with lies and threaten us with violence.
They repay the good we do for them with evil.
When they were not well, we showed great concern for them.
We prayed for them from our hearts, grieved over them with pain.
But they took advantage of our weakness with glee.
They still gather together against us.
They cripple us with unceasing slander, maim us with wounding words.
They scorn us more and more, making angry threats when we protest.

How long, O God, will You look on?
When will You rescue our lives from their ravages?
When will You save our bodies from these beasts?
When can we thank You in the congregation,
    offer praise to You among all the people?
Do not let those who wrongfully attack us continue to triumph.
Do not let those who abuse us be treated as if their wrongdoing were trivial.
For they refuse to speak the truth.
They use deceitful schemes to keep us quiet.
They counter our truth with false accusations.

But You have seen the truth, O God!
Do not remain silent and far away!
Stir Yourself, and fight for our rights!
Defend our cause, our God and just Judge!
Vindicate us, O God, in Your justice.
Let them no longer prevail over us.
Do not let them say, "We can do whatever we desire!"
Do not let them say, "We have completely overcome them."
Let those who gloat over our calamity be put to shame!
Let those who satisfy themselves at our expense be disgraced!

But let those who desire our welfare shout for joy and be glad.
Let them say forevermore,
"Great is God, who delights in the welfare of women!"
Then we will proclaim Your justice and praise You all the day long.

Reading: Mark 5:35-43 or selection from the Appendix

Prayer: Intercession for other countries and their welfare

Benediction: May God, the loving and just Judge of all people, bless us and all who cry out for justice, tonight and always. Amen.

Friday

Confession and Lamentation before God

MORNING PRAYER

Opening:

In the morning, fill us with Your love,
and we shall live this day in joy and praise!

Hymn Prayer:

God is our refuge and our strength, our ever present aid,
and therefore, though the earth be moved, we will not be afraid;
though hills amidst the seas be cast, though foaming waters roar,
yea, though the mighty billows shake the mountains on the shore.

A river flows whose streams make glad the city of our God,
the holy place wherein our God has made Her sure abode.
Since God is in the midst of her, unmoved her walls shall stand,
For God will be her early help when trouble is at hand.

Be still and know that She is God; among the heathen She
will be exalted, and on earth shall reign eternally.

The Psalter, 1912
(text modified by author)

Psalm 25
(*This might be the prayer of an older woman being divorced by a callous and unfaithful husband.*)

I open my heart to You, O God.
I put all my trust in Your love.
Do not let me be humiliated.
Do not let my adversaries triumph over me.
Vindicate the confidence of all those who wait on You,
but shame those who deceive others without reason.

Help me to know Your ways, El Shaddai.
Lead me in Your paths, O God.
Help me to walk in Your truth.
You are the One who makes me whole.
I wait for Your help every day.
Remember to show compassion, O God,
and reveal Your lasting lovingkindness to me.

Do not remember the faults of my youth,
or recall the many ways I have sinned.
Remember me with mercy and love,
and forgive me for Your goodness' sake!
For Your Name's sake pardon my guilt,
for my sins are numerous.

God is good and upright.
She teaches sinners what is right.
She guides the humble with wisdom.
She instructs the meek in Her ways.
All Her paths are merciful and true to those who keep Her covenant.

Who are the women devoted to God?
El Shaddai shows them what to choose.
Their souls shall be filled with goodness,
and their children shall inherit the earth.
Those devoted to El Shaddai enjoy Her intimate friendship.
She reveals Herself in faithful covenant with them.

As for me, my eyes are fixed in trust on El Shaddai.
She lifts my feet out of the net of trouble.
She turns to me with the face of a friend, for She knows I am lonely.
When the troubles of my heart grow greater, She delivers me from distress.
She looks on my pain and affliction, and forgives all my sins.

She considers the many obstacles I face,
    the pain of mistreatment I endure.
She keeps my soul safe and delivers me.
I am not let down when I trust in Her.
In generosity and justice God will care for me,
    for I wait on Her every day.
El Shaddai redeems me from all my distress!

Psalm 102

*(This might be the prayer of a woman suffering
from a serious chronic disease.)*

El Shaddai, hear my cry, and let my prayer come home to Your heart.
Do not hide Your face from me in my distress!
Open Your ears to my call and answer me quickly.
For my days dwindle like smoke, and my bones ache and burn.
My heart withers within me like mown grass.
I forget to eat my food.
When I groan loudly, my flesh strains against my bones.
I am like an owl in the wilderness, an owl which lives in the desert.
I keep my lonely watch like a solitary bird on a housetop.
All day long this enemy of disease ravages my well-being.
Food tastes like ashes, and I mingle my tears with my drink.
Why has this happened? Are You angry with me?
It seems You have abandoned me, have cruelly tossed me away.
My days are like a fleeting shadow.
I wither away like cut wild flowers.

But You, El Shaddai, live forever.
Every generation remembers You.
Will You arise and have mercy on me?
Has the time of Your favor come?
You have broken my strength in mid-life!

Your hand has shortened my days.
O God, do not take me away from this life so soon,
You whose years last through all generations!

You founded the earth in ages past.
The heavens are Your handiwork.
Though they will perish, You will endure.
They will wear out like old clothes,
and You will change them like garments.
But Your years have no end.

Nations of the earth, rulers of the earth,
stand and revere God's name!
For She builds up Her people in strength,
and appears among them in glory.
She listens to the pleas of the destitute.
She takes their petitions to heart.
From Her holy outlook, She sees the whole earth,
and hears all those who groan in pain.
She sets those free who are doomed to die,
so that they may proclaim Her name,
so that they may sing Her praise when the people gather in worship.

Reading: Luke 22:24-27 or selection from the Appendix

Prayer: Intercession for the world and for justice and mercy, especially for
its women

Benediction: May God bless and nourish us and all who are in need today
with Her strength in our weakness,
wih Her compassion in our failure,
and with Her comfort in our distress. Amen.

MIDDAY PRAYER

Opening:

    O God, make speed to save us!
    O Holy One, make haste to help us!

Psalm 38
*(This might be the prayer of a woman who
feels overwhelmed by sin and shortcomings.)*

    Why do You rebuke me in anger, O God?
    Why do You chasten me in Your fury?
    Your arrows wound me; Your hand lies heavy upon me.
    There is no soundness in me because of Your wrath.
    There is no health in my body because of my sins.
    I am over my head in guilt;
    my faults are a burden too heavy for me.
    I am wounded by my own foolishness.
    I am utterly bowed down with grief,
    bent over, stricken with sorrow.
    My soul is sick, and I am completely crushed.
    I moan in pain because my heart is full of turmoil.

    My God, You know my longings.
    My sighs are no secret to You.
    My heart is weak, and my strength deserts me.
    The light in my eyes is snuffed out.
    The sickness of my soul drives my friends away.
    My neighbors and family keep their distance.

    There are many who care nothing for my life.
    Others seek to hurt me, to trap me in their deceit.
    But I turn a deaf ear and keep my mouth shut.
    I act like a deaf and dumb person.

    Meanwhile, I wait for You, O God.
    How I hope You will come to my aid!
    Do not let my calamity defeat me.

I am in constant pain, ready to sink to the depths.
I confess my foolishness and am truly sorry for my sin.
Still, my demons are strong and lively, while I am weak and anxious.
I am hurt by those who treat me with dishonesty,
though they think they are doing right.
Though I am good to them, their words and deeds do me wrong.
My efforts to do what is right seem useless.

Do not forsake me, O God.
Stay close to me and help me!
You are my only hope for healing and salvation!

Psalm 39
*(This might be the prayer of a woman
feeling bitter against God.)*

This was my goal:
 "I will try to keep my tongue from speaking sinful words," I said.
 "When those who scorn me come near, I will muzzle my mouth."

So I tried to keep still, as if dumb.
I kept silent, but to no avail.
My pain was stirred up, and my heart burned within me.
My thoughts scorched me like fire.
Finally I spoke to El Shaddai:
 "O God, why am I alive? How long do I have to live?
 I know how fleeting my life is!
 My days are no greater than the breadth of a hand.
 In your eyes my life is but a moment."

Surely everyone's life is as short as a breath.
All of us are like walking shadows.
All of our turmoil is in vain.
We heap up possessions, not knowing who will get them.

O God, what is there for me to wait for?
Can I still hope in You?
Will You really save me from sin?
What about those foolish people who scorn me?

In the face of what You have done to me,
I have nothing to say, no answer to give them.
Stop punishing me, I pray.
The constant blows of Your hand are destroying me.
Your chastisement consumes what I cling to.
I am burned like a moth in a flame.
Surely I am nothing more than a breath!

Hear my prayer and answer it, O God.
Do not be silent in the face of my tears!
For my time here is short, like the stay of a guest.
Stop treating me this way, I beseech you.
I want to know some joy before my journey's end.

Silence

Prayer of the Faithful:

O God, I come before You as an empty vessel that needs filling.
My faith is weak; make it strong.
My love is cold; grant me ardor and warmth that I may love my neighbor.
I lack a vibrant and unshakable faith; sometimes I even have doubts,
and I cannot trust completely in You.
O God, come to my aid.
Increase my faith and hope in You.
I have placed in You all the riches that I possess.
I am poor, but You are rich, and You came to show mercy to the poor.
I am a sinner, but You are just.
I am filled with sin, but You are full of justice.
Hence, I will remain with You and receive from You,
although I can give You nothing.

Martin Luther, 1483-1546

O Ruler of the world, I am not asking You to show me
the secret of Your ways,
for it would be too much for me.
But I am asking You to show me one thing:
what is the meaning of the suffering that I am presently enduring,
what this suffering requires of me,

and what You are communicating to me through it.
I want to know, not so much why I am suffering,
but whether I am doing so for Your sake.

Levi Isaac of Berdichev, 1740-1809

Benediction: May the comfort and compassion of God bless us in all our foolish-ness and sorrow, that we may learn to walk in Her paths of love always. Amen.

EVENING PRAYER

Opening:

Let Your servants now rest in peace, O God,
for our eyes have seen Your salvation.

Hymn Prayer:

Out of the depths to You I raise the voice of lamentation;
God, turn a gracious ear to me, and hear my supplication;
if You would be extreme to mark each secret sin and misdeed dark,
O who could stand before You?

To wash away the crimson stain — grace, grace alone prevaileth;
our works, alas! are all in vain; in much the best life faileth;
for none can glory in Your sight; all must alike confess You right,
and live alone by Mercy.

I put my trust in God alone, and not in my own merit;
on God my soul shall rest: God's Word upholds my fainting spirit;
God's promised mercy is my strength, my comfort, and my strong support;
I wait for it with patience.

What though I wait the live-long night, and till the dawn appeareth,
my heart still trusteth in God's might; it doubteth not nor feareth:
so let the penitent in heart, born of the Spirit, do their part,
and wait till God appeareth.

Martin Luther, 1524;
translated (largely) by R. Massie, 1854
(text modified by author)

Psalm 88:1-12

*(This might be the prayer of a woman
who feels abandoned by God.)*

O God, I cry to You day and night!
Will You listen to my prayer?
My soul cries out, full of pain.
I feel that my life has come to an end.
I might as well be dead.
There is no strength or joy left within me.
I am forgotten as if I were long dead.
Do You remember those who lie in the grave?
Am I, with them, cut off from Your help?

You have thrust me into a pit of deep darkness.
Sorrow overwhelms me, sweeping over me in monstrous waves.
You have taken my loved ones away from me;
they shun me like a pariah.
I am walled up in my grief, without escape.
My eyes are blurred with tears.

Every day I call upon You, O God.
I stretch out my arms to You, pleading for help.
Do You work wonders for the dead?
Will they rise and give You thanks?
Do those in the grave proclaim Your mercy?
Do those without breath declare Your faithfulness?
Are Your wonders known in the darkness?
Is Your generosity known in the land of the dead?

Psalm 137
(This might be the prayer of women driven or taken
from their homes by warfare and violence.)

We sit down and weep beside strange streams in a strange land.
We remember our homes and sing of them under protest,
for our captors demand songs of us.
Those who torment us require cheer, saying,
"Sing us one of the songs of your homeland."

How can we sing the songs of home when we are so far away?
But, dispirited or not, we will remember our homeland!
Though our limbs wither and our tongues stick to the roof of our mouths,
we will remember our heritage, and keep it as our greatest joy!

O God, remember the way violent soldiers ruined our cities and homes.
They razed them to the foundations!
Happy are those who repay them for their devastation,
for dashing our small children on the rocks!

Reading: John 11:17-27 or selection from the Appendix

Prayer: Intercession for all the world's children and for a future of peace and plenty for them

Benediction: May the God who rescues those in great distress grant the blessing of peace to all who suffer, and keep us through this night in Her love. Amen.

Saturday

Praising God the Creator

MORNING PRAYER

Opening:

In the morning, fill us with Your love,
and we shall live this day in joy and praise!

Hymn Prayer:

This is my Mother's world, and to my listening ears
all nature sings, and round me rings the music of the spheres.
This is my Mother's world; I rest me in the thought
of rocks and trees, of skies and seas; Her hand the wonders wrought.

This is my Mother's world; the birds their carols raise;
the morning light, the lily white, declare their Maker's praise.
This is my Mother's world: She shines in all that's fair!
In the rustling grass I hear Her pass; She speaks to me everywhere!

Maltbie D. Babcock, 1901
(text modified by author)

Psalm 65
*(This might be the prayer of the many
women who farm the earth.)*

All Your people owe You praise, El Shaddai!
All flesh should pay their vows to You.
For You answer our prayer and forgive our sins,
even when they overcome us.

Blessed are those You draw near to Yourself.
They abide in Your presence,
and are satisfied with Your goodness.

You deliver us with awesome deeds, O God of our salvation.
You inspire hope to the ends of the earth, to the farthest seas.
By Your strength You set the mountains in place.
They are the earth's mighty girdle!
You still the roaring waves of the sea,
and calm the tumult of the peoples.
Those who dwell in remote places revere Your signs —
the joyful comings of morning and evening,
the beauty of sunrise and sunset.

You visit the earth with rain and nurture its soil.
You fill the rivers with swift-flowing water.
In Your generous providence You grant grain in abundance.
You settle and soften rich furrows with showers.
You water the ground and bless the land with new growth.
You crown each year with Your bountiful goodness.
Great plenty springs up in the wake of your footsteps!
The pastures of the wilderness drip with dew.
The hills are clothed with green gladness.
The meadows are filled with flocks.
The valleys are covered with grain.
Everything sings and dances together with joy,
celebrating Your bounty.

Reading: Genesis 1:26-31 or selection from the Appendix

Prayer: Intercession for all creation, the environment, all creatures, the earth itself

Benediction: May God, our Creator, Provider, and Sustainer, bless us throughout this day with the beauty and plenty She keeps on creating for our good. Amen.

MIDDAY PRAYER

Opening:

You are worthy of all praise, O God,
for You have created and are creating all things,
and for Your glory they are created!

Psalm 95:1-7

Come and sing for joy to El Shaddai!
Shout praises to the Rock of our salvation!
Come into Her holy presence with thanksgiving,
for God is great, and Her power exceeds all others!
She holds the earth in Her hands,
from its far heights to its deep places.
The sea is Hers, for She brought it forth.
With Her hands She formed the masses of land.
Come and worship Her, bow down before Her,
for El Shaddai is our God,
and we are the people She lovingly guides and cares for.

Psalm 96
(This might be the prayer of women leading worship.)

O sing a new song to El Shaddai!
Sing to God, everyone on earth!

Praise Her and bless Her name;
tell of Her salvation from day to day!
Declare Her glory among all the nations!
Proclaim Her wonders among all people!
For our God is great and deserves great praises!
Revere Her above all false powers and values,
   the vain idols of human making.
It is El Shaddai who made the heavens!
Honor and majesty are Her robes.
Beauty and strength dwell in Her presence.

Ascribe to El Shaddai all glory and power, all you families of earth.
Render to Her the glory that is Her due.
Come into Her presence with gifts of love.
Worship El Shaddai in the beauty of holiness.
Let all the earth tremble in awe before Her!
Say among the nations, "El Shaddai reigns!
She has established the earth so that it can never be moved,
and She judges all people with justice."
Let the heavens be glad and the earth dance for joy!
Let the waves of the sea roar in their splendor!
Let the fields sing for joy, and the trees clap their hands!
For El Shaddai is coming!
She comes to judge the earth in justice and generosity.
She comes to all people with Her truth.

Prayer of the Faithful:

O flaming Mountain, O chosen Sun, O full Moon,
O bottomless Well, O unattainable Height,
O Brightness beyond compare, O Wisdom without measure,
O Mercy unsurpassed, O Might irresistible,
O Crown of all glory: Your lowly creature sings Your praises.

Mechthild of Magdeburg, 1210-1282

Benediction: May God the Creator bless us with the gift of Her creativity and the sense to gently tend Her creation, that it may be renewed and restored according to Her desires. Amen.

EVENING PRAYER

Opening:

Let Your servants now rest in peace, O God,
for our eyes have seen Your salvation.

Hymn Prayer:

Immortal, invisible, God only wise,
in light inaccessible hid from our eyes,
most blessed, most beauteous, the Ancient of Days,
all loving, all glorious, Thy great name we praise!

To all life Thou givest, to all great and small;
in all life Thou livest, Thou true Life of all;
we blossom and flourish like leaves on the tree,
and wither and perish, but nought changeth Thee!

Great Mother of glory, Creator of light,
Thine angels adore Thee, all veiling their sight.
All praise we would offer; O help us to see
'tis only the splendor of light hideth Thee!

Walter Chalmers Smith, 1867
(text modified by author)

Psalm 93
(This might be the prayer of a woman scientist.)

God reigns, robed in majesty, and clothed with strong Love.
She has established the world so that it cannot be shaken.
She has existed from time's beginning,
    and Her rule is from everlasting to everlasting.

The floods of God have raised their voice.
The roaring of their waters is mightier than thunder.
But El Shaddai is greater than the thunder of many waterfalls.
She is mightier than the mightiest waves of the sea.

Her decrees are trustworthy and sure.
Her holy presence calls for holy response, now and forevermore.

Psalm 147
(This might be the prayer of women pacifists or environmentalists.)

Alleluia! It is fitting and delightful to sing praise to God.
For El Shaddai builds up Her people, and gathers the outcasts in.
She heals the brokenhearted, gently binding their wounds.
She counts the stars and calls them by name!
How great is God, abundant in powerful love!
Her wisdom is beyond all telling.

El Shaddai relieves the afflicted, breaking the power of the wicked.
Sing with thanksgiving; make melody in praise of Her!
She covers the sky with clouds, sending rain to nourish the grass.
With Her bounty She feeds the birds and beasts.

She takes no delight in the strength of arms,
no pleasure in war-like ability.
She delights in those devoted to Her, who hope in Her faithful love.

Praise El Shaddai, O people of God!
She strengthens the gates of protection.
She blesses your children among you.
She makes peace within your borders.
She fills you with the finest wheat.
She sends Her commands into all the world.
Her Word runs with the swiftness of a change in season.
She sends snow as white as wool and scatters frost like ashes.
She throws out ice like crumbs.
Who can withstand Her cold?
She sends forth Her command and melts the ice and snow.
She sets the winds blowing and the waters flowing.
She makes Her Word known to Her people — all Her desires and designs.
She favors those who follow Her will.
Alleluia!

Reading: Proverbs 31:10-31 or selection from the Appendix

Prayer: Intercession for human creativity, the arts, all artists, and the flourishing of beauty in every part of every society

Benediction: God bless you and keep you.
God make Her face shine upon you and be gracious to you.
God lift up the light of Her face upon you and give you peace! Amen.

Week Three

Sunday

Worshiping God Our Savior

MORNING PRAYER

Opening:

O God, open my lips,
and my mouth shall proclaim Your praise!

Hymn Prayer:

Holy, holy, holy! God of all glory!
Early in the morning our song shall rise to Thee.
Holy, holy, holy! Merciful and mighty!
God in three Persons, blessed Trinity!

Holy, holy, holy! All the saints adore Thee,
casting down their golden crowns upon the glassy sea.
Cherubim and seraphim bowing down before Thee,
who wert and art and evermore shalt be.

Holy, holy, holy! God of all beauty!
All Thy works shall praise Thy name in earth and sky and sea!
Only Thou art holy; there is none beside Thee,
perfect in justice, love, and purity.

Reginald Heber, 1827
(text modified by author)

Psalm 47

*(This might be the song of future women celebrating
partnership in power with men within the reign of God.)*

Clap your hands, all you women!
Sing to God with songs of joy!
For El Shaddai reigns over all the earth.
She subdues those who resist us,
    putting whole nations in our care.
She chose as our heritage the women who went before us,
    honored by God and beloved.

El Shaddai comes to the sound of glad shouts and music!
Everyone sings Her praises!
Her Love is sovereign in all the earth.
Sing psalms to celebrate Her gentle reign!
Holiness is the seat of Her authority!

The daughters of the God of Sarah gather as leaders together.
They deliver all the weapons of the earth to God.
She alone is exalted!

Psalm 48

(This might be the prayer of praise of women gathered for worship.)

El Shaddai is great, and greatly to be praised within Her holy city.
The place where Her glory dwells is the joy of all the earth.
We take refuge in the presence of God within our inner citadels.
When attackers come against us, they will be astounded.
They will flee in trembling panic.
They will cry out with the anguish of a woman in labor.
What we see verifies what we have heard:
    that El Shaddai establishes Her city forever.

We ponder Your lovingkindness, O God, within Your holy temple.
We see that the praise of Your name reaches to the ends of the earth.
Your right hand is filled with generosity.
We, Your daughters, rejoice in Your constant justice.
We walk within Your holy city, surveying Your dwelling place.

We count her towers and assess her defenses.
We tell the next generation that God is dwelling in and among us.
This God is our God forever, and will guide us even beyond death!

Psalm 87:1-3, 5, 7

The holy city of God is founded on the holy mountain.
It is the place God loves best to dwell.
Glorious things are said of you, O city of God!
God has established you firmly. . . .
We sing and dance as we cry,
"All our wellsprings are in you."

Reading: John 3:13-22; John 4:19-26; 1 Corinthians 6:12-20 or selection from the Appendix

Prayer: Intercession for the local church

Benediction: May the holiness of God's Spirit, who dwells within us, make each of us, and all of us together, a fit temple and a holy city for Her habitation! Amen.

MIDDAY PRAYER

Opening:

O God, You are our light and our salvation.
Of whom shall we be afraid?

Psalm 30
(This might be the prayer of a woman healed of addiction.)

I praise You, O God, for lifting me up and rescuing me from my foes.
When I cried to You, You heard and healed me.
You rescued my soul from hell.
You kept me alive, drawing me out of the pit of darkness.

Sing praise to God with me, all you faithful!
Give thanks for Her holy love!
Though She may be angry for a moment,
Her favor lasts forever!
The night may be filled with weeping,
but joy dawns in the morning!

As for me, I was complacent, boasting, "I shall never be moved!
God has made me as strong and secure as a mountain!"

But then You hid Your face from me, and I was filled with dismay.
I pleaded with You, El Shaddai, saying,
"Will my death profit You?
If I die will my dust be grateful to You?
Will my corpse declare Your truth?
Hear me, O God my helper. Favor and befriend me!"

You heard me, and turned my mourning to dancing!
You removed my rags of sorrow and gave me garments of gladness!
Therefore I will praise You with glory in my soul.
El Shaddai, I will never stop offering You my thanks!

Psalm 100
(This might be a woman choir director's prayer.)

Let everything in all the earth praise God with a joyful noise!
Let everyone in all the earth serve our God with gladness!

Let us come into Her presence with singing,
for we know that El Shaddai is God.
She created us; we did not create ourselves.
We are Her children, the flock She tenderly shepherds.

Enter Her house with thanksgiving!
Come into Her presence with praise!
Bless Her name with grateful hearts!
For She is good, and Her mercy endures forever.
Her faithful love enfolds every generation.

116

Prayer of the Faithful:

O God, source of everything divine,
You are good surpassing everything good, and just surpassing everything just.
In You is tranquility, as well as peace and harmony.
Heal our divisions and restore us to the unity of love
which is similar to Your divine nature.

Let the bonds of love and the ties of divine affection
make us one in the Spirit by Your peace
which renders everything peaceful.

St. Dionysius of Alexandria, c. 200-265

Benediction: May God's blessing this day turn our mourning into dancing, clothe us with peace and gladness, and set us singing with joy even when troubles assail us! Amen.

EVENING PRAYER

Opening:

Into Your hands, O God,
I commit my spirit.

Hymn Prayer:

Day is dying in the west; heaven is touching earth with rest;
wait and worship while the night sets her evening lamps alight
through all the sky.
Holy, holy, holy, Godmother of all!
Heaven and earth are full of Thee! Heaven and earth are praising Thee!
O God most nigh!

God of life, beneath the dome of the universe, Thy home,
through the glory and the grace of the stars that veil Thy face,

our prayers ascend.
Holy, holy, holy, Godmother of all!
Heaven and earth are full of Thee! Heaven and earth are praising Thee!
O God most nigh!

While the deepening shadows fall, Heart of Love enfolding all,
Gather us who seek Thy face in the folds of Thy embrace,
for Thou art nigh!
Holy, holy, holy, Godmother of all!
Heaven and earth are full of Thee! Heaven and earth are praising Thee!
O God most nigh!

Mary A. Lathbury, 1878
(text modified by author)

Psalm 50

(This might be the prayer of a prophetic woman.)

From the rising of the sun to its setting, God calls to the earth.
Out of Her holy dwelling, glorious in beauty, God shines forth.
Our God is coming, no longer keeping silent.
A purifying fire prepares Her way;
a mighty wind surrounds Her.
She calls to heaven and earth to witness Her judgments:
"Let us gather My people, who keep covenant through sacrifice."
When God Herself is judge, the very heavens declare Her righteousness!
God has this to say to Her people:
"Hear me when I speak, O My people.
I, your God, bear witness against you.
Though I do not reprove you for your sacrifices —
the things you constantly offer Me —
I have no need of the things you give.
For all the treasures of the earth are Mine.
The world and everything in it belongs to Me!
Do you think I need what you offer Me?
Do I spend money or live confined in the sanctuaries you build?
I prefer that your sacrifice be the gift of gratitude to Me,
and the keeping of your solemn promises!
Then I will save you in the day of distress,
and you will glorify Me."

118

To the careless, God has this to say:

"You have no right to recite My commands
or take My name on your lips!
For you reject My discipline and throw My words away.
You are friendly with thieves and keep company with adulterers.
Your mouths speak evil, and your tongues utter deceit.
You sit and slander the people you know.
You cruelly criticize those close to you.
Because I have been silent in the face of your misdeeds,
        you thought I was like you!
But now I bring these charges against you.
You who forgot Me, attend to Me now, for I alone can save you!
If you honor Me with those who offer Me thanksgiving,
and live by My commandments,
I will grant you My salvation!"

Psalm 150
(This might be the call to worship of a woman minister of music.)

Alleluia! Praise El Shaddai in Her holy place!
Praise Her mighty love!
Praise Her for Her saving acts!
Praise Her for Her great and generous goodness!
Praise Her with the call of the trumpet!
Praise Her with piano and guitar!
Praise Her with tambourine and dancing!
Praise Her with strings and woodwinds!
Praise Her on the drums!
Praise Her with resounding cymbals!
Let everything that breathes praise El Shaddai!
Alleluia!

Reading: Luke 1:26-38 or selection from the Appendix

Prayer: Intercession for the church worldwide, especially its unity

Benediction: May the God of music and dancing, of holiness and love, bless us through the night and this coming week with the joy and strength of Her presence! Amen.

Monday

Hoping in God Our Future

MORNING PRAYER

Opening:

O God, open my lips,
and my mouth shall proclaim Your praise!

Hymn Prayer:

All who, with heart confiding, depend on God alone,
like Zion's mount abiding, shall not be overthrown.
Like Zion's city, bounded by guarding mountains broad,
Her people are surrounded forever by their God.

No scepter of oppression shall hold unbroken sway,
lest unto base transgression the righteous turn away. . . .
From sin your saints defending, their joy, O Lord, increase,
with mercy never ending, and everlasting peace.

Psalm 125, appearing in verse form in *The Psalter*, 1912
(text modified by author)

Psalm 40

*(This might be the prayer of a woman who
escaped an abusive marriage.)*

When I waited patiently for El Shaddai, She listened, and answered my cry.
She drew me up from the pit in which I was mired.
She pulled me out of the bog in which I was trapped.
She set my feet on a rock and made my way secure.
She gave me a new song to sing — a joyful song of praise!
Many have seen this and turned in trust to Her.

Blessed are the women who trust in God,
who do not trust the proud or follow false leaders.
God has done great things for us all,
and Her works and designs are marvelous!
None can compare with El Shaddai!
To tell all Her goodness would be utterly beyond me.

She does not demand sacrifices and offerings to buy Her favor!
She opens our ears and our hearts, and longs to hear us say,
"Here I am as a sacrifice to You, O God!
I delight in doing Your will!
Your law is written on my heart,
Your desires in the book of my being."

I have proclaimed Your justice and goodness to great assemblies.
You know, O God, that I cannot restrain my lips.
I have never made a secret of Your saving help!
I speak out and proclaim Your saving faithfulness!
I do not conceal Your love or truth from any congregation.

Do not withhold Your tender mercies from me.
In lovingkindness and faithfulness keep constant watch over me.
When so many evils surround me that I cannot look up,
when I am held in the grip of sins more than the hairs on my head,
be pleased, El Shaddai, to hasten to help me!
Foil and frustrate all that seeks to destroy my soul.
Drive away all my troubles and those who delight in them!
May those who taunt me be thoroughly ashamed!

121

But let all who seek You experience Your grace,
and rejoice in Your saving presence.
Let all those who love Your holiness magnify You.
When I am poor and needy, I know You will remember me,
for You are my helper and deliverer, O God.
Please! Do not delay!

Psalm 97

(This might be the prayer of a woman missionary.)

The earth dances with joy and the islands sing, for El Shaddai reigns!
She rules justly and generously.
Darkness and clouds are Her canopy.
Purifying fire prepares for Her coming, consuming all opposition.
She illumines the world with lightning.
When the earth sees Her power, it trembles in awe.
The mountains melt in Her presence.
The heavens shine with Her beauty and order.
The peoples declare Her glory.
Those who served false images of Her are ashamed.
Those who idolatrously exalted themselves are confounded.
For all powers in heaven and earth bow down to Her.

When God's people see this, they are glad!
Their daughters and sons in all lands rejoice.
They exalt Her justice and Her power above all other powers.

God loves those who hate evil.
She guards the lives of the faithful, delivering them from destruction.
She gives light to the generous and just, and fills the upright with joy.

Rejoice in God, all you who love Her, and give thanks to Her holy name!

Reading: Galatians 3:21-28 or selection from the Appendix

Prayer: Intercession for members of the immediate family

Benediction: May the blessing of God, whose power is able to overcome all sin and evil, fill our hearts this day with overflowing hope! Amen.

MIDDAY PRAYER

Opening:

O God, You are our light and our salvation.
Of whom shall we be afraid?

Psalm 20
(This might be the prayer women offer on each other's behalf.)

In the day of trouble, may God always answer you.
May you always find protection in Her presence!
May She send you help from Her holy dwelling-place,
and support and uphold you from Her abode within you.
May She remember and accept the sacrifice of love you offer Her.
May She give you your heart's deepest desires,
and in Her wisdom fulfill all your dreams.
May you shout for joy in your successes,
and glorify Her name in your victories.
May God answer all of your prayers for good!

We know that God helps Her chosen ones,
answering them from Her holy dwelling within them.
She gives them victory with the strength of Her right hand.

Some trust in force and the power of weapons.
But we will trust in the name of our God.
When human power collapses, we will rise up in righteousness!

Silence

Prayer of the Faithful:

Holy Christ Child,
You smile sunrise into the sky.
You laugh the flowers into bloom.
Your holy play brings this day into being,
and renews all creation.
I come to You in trust like a little child.
I breathe Your love deeply into my being.
I see You in all with a child's wondering eyes.
And I ask You, Divine Child, to let me play this day with You,
laughing, trusting, delighting, creating;
and so by Your grace, with great gladness,
enter the realm of Heaven. Amen.

Anonymous, 20th century

Benediction: May the blessing of God, who became a little Child among us, fill us with divine creativity and hope, that our lives may be filled with the vitality and wonder of little children. Amen.

EVENING PRAYER

Opening:

Into Your hands, O God,
I commit my spirit.

Hymn Prayer:

Through the night of doubt and sorrow onward goes the pilgrim band,
singing songs of expectation, walking to the promised land.

One the light of God's own presence o'er Her ransomed people shed,
chasing far the gloom and terror, bright'ning all the path we tread.

One the object of our journey, one the faith which never tires,
one the earnest looking forward, one the hope our God inspires.

B. S. Ingemann, 1825
(text modified by author)

Psalm 63

*(This might be the prayer of a woman
on a spiritual retreat.)*

I earnestly search for You, my God.
My soul and my flesh faint with longing and thirst for You,
as parched earth cries out for a drink of rain.

I have seen Your powerful glory and love in the house of Your creation.
I praise You for Your steadfast love, which is better than life itself.
I will bless You as long as I live, my hands uplifted in praise.
My soul will feast and be satisfied as my lips sing for joy.

I remember You always, even while lying in bed.
I meditate on You through the wakeful hours of the night.
You are my helper, and I sing for joy in the shadow of Your wings.
My soul clings to You, and Your right hand holds me fast.

You destroy the forces that attack my soul;
they fall by the power of Your word.
Therefore I rejoice in You, El Shaddai,
trusting You to overcome all that is false.

Psalm 115

*(This might be the prayer of women
working for Christian unity.)*

Do not give glory to us, El Shaddai, but to Your name alone.
In spite of Your mercy and truth, people ask, "Where is their God?"
The one true God fills heaven and earth!
She does whatever She pleases.

As for human ideas and institutions, philosophies and structures —
they are the work of mere mortals.
Do they have mouths with which to speak?
Do they have eyes with which to see?
Do they have ears with which to hear?
Do they have noses with which to smell?
Do they have hands with which to feel?
Do they have feet with which to walk?
Do they have throats with which to talk?
They are so much less than human!
And those who make them and trust in them become just like them!

O people of God, trust in El Shaddai!
She is our help and our hope.
O household of priestly people, put your confidence in God!
She alone protects and saves us.
All you who revere El Shaddai, trust only in Her!
She is our helper and protector.

El Shaddai remembers us always.
She will bless the whole household of Her people.
She will bless all those who revere Her, the small and the great alike.

May God's bounty grace the lives of both you and your children!
May you be blessed by God, who brought forth the earth and the heavens!
The heavens belong to God, but the earth She has given to us all.
Therefore, bless El Shaddai, and praise Her now and forever!
Alleluia!

Reading: Romans 12:1-8 or selection from the Appendix

Prayer: Intercession for the extended family

Benediction: May the blessing of El Shaddai, our Helpmate, Protection, and Salvation, nourish your soul and restore your body, through this night and forevermore. Amen.

Tuesday

Seeking God's Wisdom

MORNING PRAYER

Opening:

O God, open my lips,
and my mouth shall proclaim Your praise!

Hymn Prayer:

Be Thou my vision, O God of my heart;
nought be all else to me, save what Thou art —
Thou my best thought, by day or by night,
waking or sleeping, Thy Presence my light.

Be Thou my Wisdom, and Thou my true Word;
I ever with Thee and Thou with me, God;
Thou my great Teacher, Thy Spirit in me;
Thou in me dwelling, and I one with Thee.

Thou and Thou only, first in my heart;
Giver of all good, my treasure Thou art;
Heart of my own heart, whatever befall,
still be my vision, Thou true Life of all.

Ancient Irish poem translated by Mary E. Byrne, 1905;
this version by Eleanor Hull, 1912

Psalm 119:57-80
(This might be the prayer of a woman
rededicating her life to God.)

El Shaddai, You are the treasure of my heart!
I promise to walk in the way of Your Word.
I long for Your favor with my whole being.
Grant me the grace You have promised!
When I thought over Your ways, I decided to seek Your wisdom.
I did not delay in trying to do Your will.
When the cords of wrongdoing ensnare me,
I will remember Your commands.
Because You are just and generous,
I will rise to praise You in the middle of the night.
My companions are those who revere You and keep Your precepts.
El Shaddai, Your steadfast love fills the whole earth!

You have been good to me according to Your promise.
Teach me Your ways and grant me good judgment.
Help me to know the meaning of Your commands,
for I believe they are true.

Suffering has taught me to keep Your Word,
and rescued me from straying.
Because You are good and do what is good,
I want to learn Your precepts.
Though the godless defame me with lies,
I will wholeheartedly walk in Your ways.
Though they treat me without feeling,
I will delight in Your will.
Affliction has been good for me,
because it has taught me the deep meanings of Your ways.
Your Wisdom has become more precious to me than much fine gold.

Help me discern Your will, for Your hands have shaped me.
You have fixed me firmly in Your love.
Because I hope in Your Word, those who love You will rejoice.
I know, El Shaddai, that Your judgments are just,
and that You have let me suffer because You care for me.
Comfort me now, I beg You, with Your unfailing compassion.

Grant me life according to Your faithful promises,
for Your desires are my delight.
Let the critical be put to shame for their heartless lying.
As for me, I will meditate always on Your precepts.
Let those who revere You join me,
that we may grow in Your wisdom together.
May our hearts be blameless in keeping Your Word.
May we never be put to shame!

Reading: Acts 1:12-14 and 2:1-4 or selection from the Appendix

Prayer: Intercession for friends and neighbors

Benediction: May the Holy Spirit of all Wisdom lead us ever more deeply into Truth, that we may walk steadfastly in Her ways of justice and love. Amen.

MIDDAY PRAYER

Opening:

O God, You are our light and our salvation.
Of whom shall we be afraid?

Psalm 119:81-112
(This might be the prayer of a woman lawyer
prosecuting corrupt government officials.)

My whole being languishes for Your holiness, O God.
I hope in Your Word to make me whole.
I strain my eyes watching for You to fulfill Your promises.
I wonder when You will comfort me.
I have become as fragile as worn-out fabric.
How long must Your servant endure?
When will You recompense those who attack me?
Godless people dig pitfalls for me.

Though they refuse to conform to Your will, I remember Your commands.
They persecute me with falsehood because I am true to Your laws.
They have almost finished me off, but I persevere in Your precepts.

Help me, and in Your mercy grant me fullness of life,
so that I may continue to keep the word You have spoken.

Your Word, O God, is fixed firmly in the heavens.
Your faithfulness extends to all generations.
You founded the earth to last through the ages.
Everything owes its existence to Your sustaining power.
Everything in all creation serves Your designs.

If I did not delight in Your will, I might have perished with grief.
Because Your precepts give me life, I will never forget them.
Save me, for I belong to You and constantly search out Your ways.
Though the wicked lie in wait to destroy me, I consider Your purposes.
There is a limit to all perfection, but Your good will exceeds it!

How I love Your wisdom! I meditate on it day and night.
Your guidance makes me wiser than my enemies.
Your truths are established within me.
Because I ponder Your ways in my heart,
I understand more than my teachers.
Because I keep Your precepts with care,
I understand more than the aged.
Your Word holds me back from evil;
You teach me how to honor Your will.

I taste Your Words and find them sweet —
sweeter than honey on the tongue!
Your precepts give me understanding.
They teach me to hate dishonesty.
Your Word is like a lamp to my feet,
like a light upon a dark path.
I vow that I will always observe Your just ways.
Now, when I am sore with suffering,
give me life through Your Word.
Accept my free offering of praise, O God,
and lead me in Your paths of wisdom.

In trying to follow Your precepts, I often take my life in my hands.
The corrupt lay traps to ensnare me, but I do not stray
     from Your commands.
Your wisdom is my heritage forever.
My heart dances with joy as I follow Your good will,
determined to take Your path to the very end!

Silence

Prayer of the Faithful:

Holy Spirit, send from heaven a spark of Your radiant heart.
Mother of the poor, bestowing gifts on those in need,
come, Source of Life, within our hearts.

Deepest source of consolation dwelling in our souls,
You give pilgrims their repose.
To the toiling You give rest;
You cool the burning heat and comfort those in tears.

O most joyful like a Bride, fill the secret hearts of those who trust in You.

Without the presence of Your Godhead,
nothing lies in us free from harm.

Wash what is soiled,
water what is dry,
heal what is wounded.
Bend what is rigid,
warm what is cold,
find what is lost.

Grant to those who believe and trust in You
the sacred gifts and fruits of love.
Grant us the reward of Your work in us.
Consummate our lives in peace,
and grant us joy forever. Alleluia!

Byzantine liturgy

Benediction: May the blessing of God, who is the Source of all Truth, all Wisdom, and all Faithfulness, help us to be true, wise, and faithful in all our ways, this day and always. Amen.

EVENING PRAYER

Opening:

Into Your hands, O God,
I commit my spirit.

Hymn Prayer:

Sing praise to God who reigns in love, the God of all creation,
the God of power, the God of love, the God of our salvation;
with healing balm my soul She fills and ev'ry faithless murmur stills:
To God all praise and glory!

What God's almighty power hath made, Her gracious mercy keepeth;
by morning glow or evening shade, Her watchful eye ne'er sleepeth.
Within Her realm of love and light, lo! all is just and all is right:
To God all praise and glory!

Our God is never far away, but through all grief distressing,
an ever-present help and stay, our peace and joy and blessing.
As with a mother's tender hand, She leads Her own, Her chosen band:
To God all praise and glory!

J. J. Schutz, 1675;
translated by Frances E. Cox, 1858
(text modified by author)

Psalm 119:113-36

(This might be the prayer of a businesswoman beset by dishonest and unfair business competitors.)

I despise dishonesty and double-dealing,
but I love Your law.
I hope in Your Word; it gives me a cloak and a covering.
But my competitors depart from You and act unjustly.
Even so, I will always try to keep Your commands, O God.
Let Your Word uphold me, that I may live wisely.
I hope in You — do not let me down!
Hold me up and save me, for I always look to Your Word.

You spurn those who spurn Your ways;
their clever cheating is in vain.
Because You count the dishonest as dross,
I love Your ways and stand trembling in awe of Your greatness.
I deeply revere Your judgments and try to do what is right.
Do not let my enemies overthrow me.
Do not abandon me to their ill treatment.
Guard my well-being in the face of their schemes.

My eyes are weary with watching for signs of Your salvation,
for the fulfillment of Your promise to uphold the just.
Deal with my efforts with patient and steadfast love.
Teach me Your will and give me true understanding.
Help me also to know Your desires and to obey You with a wise heart.
I am trying to serve You; help me to understand how.
O God, it is high time for You to act!
See how Your will is flouted!

As for me, I find Your precepts far more precious than gold.
I love what You command and hate every false way.
Your designs are wonderful.
I ponder them deep in my being.
Your Word brings light when it enters my heart.
Though I am simple, it makes me wise.
My mouth pants with longing for Your wisdom.
Be gracious to me, for I am faithful to You.

Fix my steps in Your paths and do not let evil sway me.
Free me from the depression of despair.
My eyes stream with tears because of those who forsake You.
Make Your face shine on me and comfort me with Your truth.

Reading: Acts 2:14-21 or selection from the Appendix

Prayer: Intercession for enemies/adversaries/competitors

Benediction: May the blessing of God enable you to rest in Her Wisdom and Word this night and always. Amen.

Wednesday

Trusting in God Our Refuge

MORNING PRAYER

Opening:

O God, open my lips,
and my mouth shall proclaim Your praise!

Hymn Prayer:

O grant us light, that we may know the wisdom Thou alone canst give,
that truth may guide where'er we go, and virtue bless where'er we live.

O grant us light, that we may learn how dead is life from Thee apart,
how sure is joy for all who turn to Thee with undivided heart.

O grant us light, in grief and pain, to give our burdens unto Thee,
and count the suffering a gain, and bless Thy wisdom's true mercy.

Lawrence Tuttiett, 1864

Psalm 34
(This might be the prayer of a mother teaching her faith to her daughters and sons.)

I will bless and praise El Shaddai continually!
I will glory in God.
Little ones will hear me with gladness.
They will magnify El Shaddai with me,
and we will exalt Her name together!

When I sought God, She came to me.
She delivered me from all my fears.
Your crestfallen faces will shine with radiance
when you look to Her in faith.

When a poor woman cries, God hears her.
El Shaddai saves her through and in all her troubles.
The angel of El Shaddai's presence surrounds all those who trust Her.
She saves them from all their difficulties.
O taste and see how good God is!
Blessed are the women who take refuge in Her!
Those who revere El Shaddai will lack nothing they need.
Though young lions may suffer hunger,
the faithful will be satisfied with God's goodness.

Come, children, listen to me.
I will teach you to love El Shaddai!
Do you desire to live a long and full life?
Do you want to experience its goodness?
Then keep your tongues from being destructive,
your lips from speaking lies.
Depart from evil and do what is good.
Always seek peace — pursue it!

God watches the faithful with loving eyes.
Her ears are always attuned to their cry.
But She turns Her back on those who do evil.
She erases their memory from the earth.
When the just cry for help, God hears and delivers them.
She makes the brokenhearted whole.
She sustains and saves those whose spirits are crushed.

When the faithful suffer much evil,
El Shaddai delivers them from it all.
She preserves their spirits from harm.

The wicked will be overcome by the evil they do;
those who oppose the just will be held guilty.
El Shaddai redeems those who love and serve Her.
None who take refuge in Her will ever be condemned!

Reading: John 4:1-26, 39-42 or selection from the Appendix

Prayer: Intercession for the local community, town, or city

Benediction: May the blessing of God be our refuge today and always. Amen.

MIDDAY PRAYER

Opening:

O God, You are our light and our salvation.
Of whom shall we be afraid?

Psalm 112
(This might be the prayerful instruction
of a godly grandmother.)

Blessed is the woman who reveres El Shaddai,
who takes great delight in Her will.
Her descendants will be great in the land;
Her upright offspring will flourish.
Wealth and well-being are in her house.
Her justice and generosity will never grow old.
Light dawns in the darkness for the upright —
the gracious, compassionate, and just.
It goes well for the generous woman,
she who lends freely to the needy,

who conducts her affairs with justice.
The righteous woman will never be shaken.
She will always be remembered.
She is not afraid of bad news,
because her heart is firmly moored in God.
She is steadfast and unafraid within,
even when confronted by trouble.
She distributes her goods freely to the poor.
Because of her constant uprightness, she is held in great honor.

The hard-hearted and unjust are angered by this,
but their threats come to nothing.
Their selfish desires are frustrated.

Psalm 131
*(This might be the prayer of a woman
scholar and professor.)*

El Shaddai, I want to avoid arrogance.
I do not want to walk in ways too difficult for me,
or try to understand things beyond my grasp.
I calm myself now and sit quietly in Your embrace,
like a weaned child at its mother's breast,
my soul like a tranquil little one.
With Your people, I hope in You, now and forevermore.

Silence

Prayer of the Faithful:

O God, I come before You with full awareness of all my weaknesses
and in total awe of Your greatness and majesty.
But You want me to pray to You and to revere Your exalted name
in accord with the limits of my understanding.

You have the best knowledge of the things that are for my good.
I give expression to my needs not to recall them to You,
but solely to get a better understanding of my utter dependence on You.

Therefore, if I petition You for something that is not good for me,
it is only out of ignorance.
You are in a far better position than I am to choose what to grant me.
I submit myself completely to Your decisions
and to Your guidance, which knows no equal.

Bachya Pakudah, 1000-1080

Benediction: May the blessing of God be our refuge in all the difficulties of our
day and our life. Amen.

EVENING PRAYER

Opening:

Into Your hands, O God,
I commit my spirit.

Hymn Prayer:

God, that madest earth and heaven, darkness and light,
who the day for toil hast given, for rest the night:
may Thine angels guard, defend us, slumber sweet Thy mercy send us;
holy dreams and hopes attend us, this live-long night.

When the constant sun returning unseals our eyes,
may we, born anew like morning, to labor rise.
Gird us for the task that calls us, let not selfish ways enthrall us,
strong through Thee whate'er befall us, O God most wise!

Reginald Heber, stanza 1, 1827;
and Frederick Hosmer, stanza 2, 1912

Psalm 94

*(This might be the prayer of women
protesting injustice and violence.)*

El Shaddai, let Your justice shine out!
O Judge of all the earth, rise up and deal with proud oppressors!
How long, O God, will You let the wicked triumph?
They speak impudently and boast tirelessly.
They crush Your people, O God, and afflict Your beloved heritage.
They attack defenseless women and strangers;
they destroy innocent children.
"Who cares?" they say scornfully. "God does not see!"

Listen, you foolish leaders! Be wise, you brutish oppressors!
Does She who formed the ear not hear?
Does She who shaped the eye not see?
Does She who rules the nations not chastise their evil?
Does She who gives people knowledge not know what they think?
Does She not see the vanity in your minds?
You will be blessed if She chastens you!
You will be wise when you do Her will.

Give Your oppressed respite in trouble, El Shaddai,
till the wicked get what they deserve!
Do not abandon Your people or let Your heritage suffer.
Let justice return to the faithful, peace to the upright in heart.

Who will rise up with us against the doers of evil?
Who will stand up with us against the corruption of the rich and powerful?
If El Shaddai does not help us, we will sink into deathly silence.

When we feel we are slipping, Her steadfast love catches us.
She holds us in Her hands, our protector in times of trouble.
When our hearts are heavy, Her comforts delight our souls.

Unjust rulers who make perverse laws cannot claim God's support!
They gather their might against the upright;
they condemn the innocent to death.
But El Shaddai is our sure rock of refuge;
She is our stronghold and mighty defense.

She will make them suffer the consequences of their sin,
will wipe out their power to harm.
El Shaddai will most surely cut them off!

Reading: 1 Kings 17:8-16; Luke 4:23-27; or selection
from the Appendix

Prayer: Intercession for the larger community, state, province, etc.

Benediction: May the God who is our Refuge, our Comfort, and our Defense bless
us through this night and always. Amen.

Thursday

Crying Out to God for Justice

MORNING PRAYER

Opening:

> O God, open my lips,
> and my mouth shall proclaim Your praise!

Hymn Prayer:

> How good it is to thank the Lord, to praise Her name with tuneful chord;
> to show Her love with morning light and tell Her faithfulness each night.
> Yes, it is good Her praise to sing and all our sweetest music bring.
>
> O God, my song with joy expands before the wonders of Your hands.
> How great the works that You have wrought; how deep,
>   O God, Your every thought!
> You make me glad; I sing Your praise for all Your wondrous
>   works and ways.
>
> O God, You have exalted me with royal strength and dignity.
> With Your anointing I am blest; Your grace and favor on me rest.
> Your foes will fall before Your might, and wickedness be put to flight.

The righteous all will flourish well and in the house of God will dwell.
They will be planted like a tree, will still in old age fruitful be.
Our God is always upright, just; She is our rock; in Her we trust.

Psalm 92, appearing in this verse form in *The Psalter*, 1912
(text modified by author)

Psalm 41

(This might be the prayer of a woman
who has been ill for a long time.)

Blessed is the woman who treats the weak wisely and well.
God will save her when evil days come.
El Shaddai will watch over her and give her life.
People will call her blessed.
God will not deliver her to her inner foes.
El Shaddai will sustain her in sickness;
She will heal her and make her strong.

Here is my prayer:
"Favor me, God, and heal me.
for I have sinned against you.
Will I die, my name be wiped out forever?
People visit me, mouthing empty words,
caring nothing for me in their hearts.
After they leave, they gossip about me.
Their hatred whispers against me.
They imagine the worst for me.
Will I ever get up from this sickbed?
Even my closest and most trusted friends have forgotten me.
I feel utterly abandoned.
Recognize my plight, El Shaddai, and be gracious to me!
Raise me up and prove that I am not wrong to trust You.
When You are by my side, my inner foes do not prevail.
Uphold me in integrity and fix me in Your love forever!"

Blessed be El Shaddai, the God of all people, now and through all ages.
Amen and Amen.

Psalm 86

*(This might be the prayer of poor women
living in oppressive countries.)*

Listen to us and speak to us, El Shaddai,
for we are poor and needy!
Preserve our souls, for we love You.
Save us, for we trust in You.

Every day we pray for Your favor.
Gladden our souls and open our hearts to You.
For You are good and fully forgiving.
You are rich in mercy to all.

Give ear to our prayer, El Shaddai!
Listen to the sound of our pleading.
We call on You in time of trouble,
for You have promised to answer us.

Among the powers that be, no other is like You.
No other's works are as wonderful as Yours.
You have created all people, all nations,
and someday they shall all serve You, El Shaddai!
They will bow down and glorify Your name!
For You are the one and only wonder-working God!
You alone are great!

Teach us Your ways, El Shaddai,
so that we may walk in Your wisdom.
Unite every part of our beings in loving devotion to You.
We will give You wholehearted thanks!
We will glorify Your name forever!
For Your steadfast love is great toward us.
You deliver our souls from hell and its darkness.

El Shaddai, oppressive people have risen against us.
Violent troops are seeking our lives.
They serve their own ends rather than You.
Gracious and loving God of our lives,
You abound in mercy and faithfulness.

Turn to us now in compassion.
Give Your strength to us, Your servants.
Save the daughters of Your faithful ones.
Show us signs of Your favor,
that those who scorn us may be ashamed.
Help us, O God, and grant us the strength and comfort we need.

Reading: Malachi 2:13-16 and Matthew 5:27-32 or selection from the Appendix

Prayer: Intercession for one's own country and its leaders

Benediction: May God grant the blessings of justice to us and to all peoples, this day and forever. Amen.

MIDDAY PRAYER

Opening:

O God, You are our light and our salvation.
Of whom shall we be afraid?

Psalm 55
(This might be the prayer of women living in violent, crime-infested neighborhoods.)

O God, listen to our prayers.
Hear our cries and stop hiding Yourself!
Be attentive to us and answer us.
We are lost in a sea of problems.
We are distraught by the crime around us,
By the wickedness we must live with.
We constantly stumble into trouble.
We are shaken and angry.
Our hearts are in anguish, gripped by pain.
We are overcome by the terror of violence and death.
We are seized with fear and trembling.
Horror overwhelms us.

O God, if only we had wings like a bird,
so we could fly away and be at rest!
We ache to be as far from this place as we can.
We wish we could flee to the wilderness.
We long to escape from the tempest of terror around us.

El Shaddai, destroy the schemes of all criminals!
Subdue the violence and strife in the city!
Day and night, violent gangs strut about the streets,
making mischief and trouble in the neighborhood.
The shopping malls and stores are filled with greed.
Guile and oppression stalk our streets.

We are not beset by strangers —
that would be more bearable.
But our adversaries are our neighbors.
They know who we are.
That makes it harder to bear!
Some of those who commit crimes were our friends.
We used to talk to each other in peace and companionship.
Some even went to God's house to worship with us!

But now the desolation of drugs stalks their dwellings.
They sink down into the pit of corruption.
Their houses are full of evil.

So we keep calling on God, trusting in Her to save us.
Morning, noon, and night we cry and complain.
She hears us and keeps our souls safe in the battle we wage.
Though many are pitted against us, God will humble them.
For they refuse to change and show Her no reverence.

Our former friends have broken their promises.
Now they stretch out their hands against us.
They speak smoothly, glibly, but violence lurks in their hearts.
Their words are like silk yet sharp like knives.
They act with cutting hostility.

We can do nothing but cast our burdens on God.
She has promised to sustain us.
She will not allow the upright to be shaken.
She will cast betrayers into the lowest pit,
cut off the lives of the violent and treacherous.
Because She upholds us, we will trust in Her.

Prayer of the Faithful:

Blessed are You, my God,
for You open Your servants' hearts to knowledge,
render all their actions just,
and accomplish for their children
the plan that You have formed
with respect to those whom You have chosen.
May they remain unceasingly in Your presence!

How can one walk a straight path without Your help?
What can one accomplish without Your accord?
From You alone comes all knowledge.
Nothing takes place except in accord with Your will.
No one but You can make answer to You,
unravel the skein of Your sacred designs,
scrutinize Your unfathomable mysteries,
or meditate on Your astounding works
and the munificence of Your power.

From the Dead Sea Scrolls, 20 B.C. to A.D. 70

Benediction: May the blessing of God enable us all to trust in Her goodness and,
in times of trouble, to flee to Her for protection. Amen.

EVENING PRAYER

Opening:

Into Your hands, O God,
I commit my spirit.

Hymn Prayer:

Praise God, you servants of the Lord, and bless Her name with one accord.
O praise our God, Her name adore from this time forth forevermore.

From rising unto setting sun praised be our God, the Mighty One.
She reigns o'er all, in love and light, and fills the heavens with glory bright.

God lifts the poor and makes them great; with joy She fills the desolate;
The barren come to motherhood. Sing hallelujah! God is good!

Psalm 113, appearing in this verse form in *The Psalter*, 1912
(text modified by author)

Psalm 56
(This might be the prayer of a woman caught in revolution.)

Deliver me, O God, before my life is snuffed out!
All day long there is fighting around me.
All day long my enemies oppress me.
The pride that fuels this fighting is everywhere.

Whenever I am afraid, I try to trust in You.
Your Word gives me confidence,
and when I praise You, I lose my fear.
Nothing can harm my soul, which is always in Your hands.

All day long people plot destruction against me.
I fear that they will destroy me.
They stir up strife wherever they go.
They watch me from hiding places, lying in wait for me.
There is no escape from their violence!

O God, cast all violent people down!
Take account of my pain and distress.
Though I bottle up my tears, I know You keep count of them.
Vanquish my enemies when I call upon You!
Let me know that You are for me, my ally in trouble.
I praise Your Word and try to trust You without fear.
What can evil people do to me as long as You protect me?
If You will deliver my body and soul from death,
I solemnly promise to offer You thanks.
Keep my feet from falling, I pray.
Let me walk before You in the light of the living.

Psalm 82
(This might be the prayer of a woman governor.)

God has taken Her place in the divine council.
She exercises judgment among the powers that be.
She says:
> "How long will you continue to be unjust,
> to give special favors to those who do evil?
> Give justice to widows and orphans, women and children.
> Rescue the needy and deliver the weak:
> free them from the power of their oppressors."

Those who wield power lack understanding;
they act in the darkness of ignorance.
Their folly shakes the foundations of the earth.

Though they act as if they were gods,
and claim to be God's favored children,
they shall die like any mortal,
shall fall like any ruler.

Rise up, El Shaddai!
Establish Your just rule in all the earth!
For the nations belong to You.

Reading: John 12:1-8 and Matthew 26:6-13 or selection from the Appendix

Prayer: Intercession for the welfare of other countries and a plea for wisdom for their leaders

Benediction: May the God of justice, mercy, and deliverance keep us from falling and fix us firmly in Her presence through this night and forever. Amen.

Friday

Confession and Lamentation before God

MORNING PRAYER

Opening:

> O God, open my lips,
> and my mouth shall proclaim Your praise!

Hymn Prayer:

> O God, Thou art my God alone; early to Thee my soul shall cry,
> a pilgrim in a land unknown, a thirsty land whose springs are dry.
>
> Yet through this rough and thorny maze I follow close to Thee, my God;
> Thy hand unseen upholds my ways; I safely tread where Thou hast trod.

> James Montgomery, 1822

Psalm 32
(This might be the prayer of a woman
who has recognized the dishonesty of her life.)

> How blessed I am! My sins are forgiven!
> My guilt is wholly removed!
> God does not condemn me, but saves me from corruption.
> She removes all guile from my spirit.

When I refused to see my sins and kept guilty silence,
I ached and groaned all day long like an aged woman.
Day and night I felt Your hand like a heavy weight on my heart.
My soul dried up and withered like plants in a drought.

Then I confessed my sin to You.
I no longer tried to cover up my guilt.
And when I confessed my transgression,
You forgave me completely!

When the godly see the dark side of themselves,
let them go to You in prayerful confession.
Then they will not be overwhelmed by floods of guilt.
They will realize with me that You are our hiding place.
In times of trouble You protect our souls,
surrounding us with songs of deliverance!
You instruct us and teach us the way we should go.
You watch over us and give us wise counsel.
You ask us not to be like horses and mules, without understanding,
who wander away if they are not held with bit and bridle.

The wicked who wander from God suffer many sorrows,
but those who trust in God are embraced by mercy.
Therefore be glad and rejoice in El Shaddai, you who love Her,
and shout for joy, all you who live with integrity!

Reading: Luke 15:8-10 or selection from the Appendix

Prayer: Intercession for the world and for justice and mercy for its women especially

Benediction: May the merciful blessing of God, who forgives our sins, restore us to wholeness and enable us to love ourselves and one another as we have been loved by God, so that we may live in the solidarity of Her embrace. Amen.

MIDDAY PRAYER

Opening:

O God, You are our light and our salvation.
Of whom shall we be afraid?

Psalm 51
(This might be the confessional prayer of any woman
or man who wants to be closer to God.)

Merciful God, be gracious to me!
Compassionate God, blot out my folly!
Wash away my guilt and sin!

I confess the wrong I have done,
and I see the ways in which I have sinned.
I acknowledge I have done what is evil in Your eyes.
I realize it is You I have offended.
You are right to reproach me,
to exercise Your just judgment upon me.

I was born with the disease of sin.
From the beginning I have been burdened with guilt.

You desire the triumph of truth within me.
Reveal Your wisdom to me in my heart's hidden chambers.
Purify my inner self, as with hyssop, and I will be clean.
Wash every part of me, and I will be white as snow.
Grant me gladness again, that this broken self may dance with joy!
Do not look at my sinfulness, I pray,
and blot out the stains of my guilt.

O God, create a clean heart in me!
Put a right and faithful spirit within me.
Do not take away the gift of Your presence.
Do not remove Your Holy Spirit from me.
Restore and heal me, that I may know the joy of wholeness.
Sustain me with Your generous spirit.

Then I will teach other transgressors Your ways,
that they may return, with me, to You.
Deliver me from being destructive, O God.
You alone can save me from my sinful behavior.

O God, open my lips, and I will proclaim Your praise!
My tongue shall sing aloud of Your loving generosity.
You do not delight in sacrifices and gifts offered to secure Your favor.
What You honor is the sacrifice of a humble spirit and a contrite heart.

Silence

Prayer of the Faithful:

O God, do not turn Your servant away.
I am sunk in the mire — grasp my hand.
Grant Your mercy in exchange for the sin I have committed.
Let Your wind sweep away the evil I have done.
Tear off my many transgressions as one tears off a garment.
My God, my sins number seven times seven; forgive all of them.

Babylonian psalm

Benediction: May God the Creator bless you with a clean heart; may God the Redeemer bless you with increasing freedom from sin; may God the Holy Spirit bless you with growing wholeness and holiness. Amen.

EVENING PRAYER

Opening:

Into Your hands, O God,
I commit my spirit.

Hymn Prayer:

Thee in the watches of the night I will remember on my bed,
Thy presence makes the darkness light; Thy guardian wings are round my
   head.

Better than life itself Thy love, dearer than all beside to me;
for whom have I in heav'n above, or what on earth, compared with Thee?

Praise with my heart, my mind, my voice, for all Thy mercy I will give;
my soul shall still in God rejoice; my tongue shall bless Thee while I live.

James Montgomery, 1822

Psalm 77
(This might be the prayer of an old woman
forsaken by her family.)

When I lift my voice and cry out to God, does She really hear me?
In days of distress I search for God.
In dark nights I pray without ceasing.
But my soul finds no comfort.
Though I remember God, I am troubled.
Though I meditate on Her, my spirit faints and fails.
In my trouble I cannot sleep.
I cannot find words to express my pain.
I consider days past and remember years gone by.
I pray with songs in my heart in the night.
My spirit is restless, searching, full of questions.
"Will God cast me away forever?
Is She displeased with me?
Has She withdrawn Her mercy from me?
Has Her promise through the generations now failed?
Has She forgotten to be gracious?
Has She in anger stopped being compassionate?
Is this why I am sick and forsaken?"

For comfort, I will remember the deeds of God through the years.
I will remember all Her wonderful works.
I will call to mind what She has done and muse on Her designs. . . .

O God, Your ways are holy.
You are great, and You have worked many wonders.
You have revealed Your purpose among the nations.
You have freed Your people with the strength of Your love.
You have redeemed the children of Sarah.
When the waters saw You, they parted in fear.
The deeps trembled, and the clouds poured rain.
The skies thundered and flashed with bolts of lightning.
The thunder of Your voice and the light of Your coming awed the world!
The earth quaked and trembled as You made Your way through the sea.
Though Your footsteps were unseen, Your path parted the great waters.
You led Your people like a flock by the hands of Miriam and Moses.

Reading: Matthew 23:37-39 or selection from the Appendix

Prayer: Intercession for all the world's children and for a future of peace and well-being for them

Benediction: May the blessing of God, who never abandons us or fails to keep Her promise, fill us with peace this night and always. Amen.

Saturday

Praising God the Creator

MORNING PRAYER

Opening:

> O God, open my lips,
> and my mouth shall proclaim Your praise!

Hymn Prayer:

> Joyful, joyful we adore Thee, God of glory, Lord of love;
> hearts unfold like flowers before Thee, opening to the sun above.
> Melt the clouds of sin and sadness, drive the dark of doubt away;
> Giver of immortal gladness, fill us with the light of day!
>
> All Thy works with joy surround Thee; earth and heaven reflect Thy rays;
> stars and angels sing around Thee, center of unbroken praise!
> Field and forest, vale and mountain, flowering meadow, flashing sea,
> chanting bird and flowing fountain call us to rejoice in Thee.
>
> Thou art giving and forgiving, ever blessing, ever blessed;
> Wellspring of the joy of living, ocean depths of happiness.
> Thou our Mother, Christ our Savior, all who live in love are Thine;
> teach us how to love each other, fill us with Thy joy divine.

Mortals, join the mighty chorus which the morning stars began!
Mother love is reigning o'er us; sister love binds hand to hand.
Ever singing, walk we onward, victors in the midst of strife;
joyful music leads us forward in the triumph song of life!

Henry Van Dyke, 1907
(text modified by author)

Psalm 74:12-17

(This might be the prayerful praise
of Jewish women on the Sabbath.)

> El Shaddai, You are our God.
> From ancient times You have worked salvation in the midst of the earth.
> You divided the sea with Your might;
> You broke the threat of watery chaos.
> You crushed the head of the monstrous Serpent;
> You nourished Your people in the desert.
> You split open fountains and torrents of springs;
> You dried up mighty rivers.
> Yours is the day and Yours is the night.
> You have made the sun, moon, and stars.
> You have fixed all the boundaries of earth.
> You sustain all the seasons.

Psalm 104

(This might be the prayerful praise
of a woman living in a rural area.)

> My whole soul blesses El Shaddai, for She is very great.
> She is robed with honor and majesty, cloaked with light.
> The heavens are Her tent,
> the waters are the foundation of Her dwelling.
> She rides on the towering clouds and walks on the wings of the wind!
> Flames of fire serve Her, and breezes carry Her messages.

She established the earth on unshakeable foundations,
covering it with deep waters.
At Her thunderous word the waters that stood above the mountaintops fled.
She made the mountains rise up and the valleys sink down,
high and low, in the places She planned for them.
She bounded the waters so they would never again cover the earth.

She sends streams flowing into the valleys between the hills.
All the wild animals quench their thirst at Her springs.
Above them, the birds sing in the trees in which they nest.
She waters the hills from Her upper rooms,
and nourishes the earth with Her goodness.
She makes grass grow for cattle and plants thrive for people to cultivate.
Women and men bring forth food from the earth:
wine to gladden their hearts,
oil to make their faces shine,
and bread to strengthen and sustain them.

The mountain cedars which El Shaddai plants are lush and full.
The birds of the air build their nests in them.
Among the fir branches the stork makes a home for her young.
In the high mountain places the wild goats roam.
Among the rocks the badgers find refuge.

El Shaddai has made the moon to mark the passing of the months.
The sun She has set in the sky knows how to mark the hours.
She makes day and night, darkness and light.
In the night the beasts of the forests creep forth,
prowling the darkness, seeking their prey.
In the morning the beasts return to their lairs,
and human beings rise up to work, toiling until evening.

The works of El Shaddai are wonderful indeed!
In Her great wisdom She has created everything.
The sea is full of Her treasures.
Deep and wide, shining on every shore,
it is filled with numberless creatures, living things great and small.
The ships ply the waters while the great sea monsters play in them.

All creatures wait for God to supply their sustenance.
She provides for them, and they gather Her bounty.
She opens Her hands and satisfies them with many good things.
If She hides Her face, they are troubled.
If She inhales in their breath, taking it into Herself,
they die and return to dust.
When She sends forth Her Spirit, She creates again;
She renews the face of the earth.
The glory of God is always shining in Her creation.
She rejoices in all Her works —
She who makes the earth tremble with a glance,
who makes the mountain heights smoke at her touch.

So I will sing praise to God every day of my life!
I will adore Her as long as I live!
How sweet is my meditation on Her!
How I love to dance for joy before El Shaddai!

Someday perversity will perish from the earth,
and wickedness will vanish forever.
Bless El Shaddai, my whole soul! Alleluia!

Reading: Proverbs 8:22-36 or selection from the Appendix

Prayer: Intercession for all creation — the environment, the earth, and all its creatures.

Benediction: May the God who creates heaven and earth bless us with increasing fruitfulness and harmony with all that She has made! Amen.

MIDDAY PRAYER

Opening:

O God, You are our light and our salvation.
Of whom shall we be afraid?

*(This might be the prayer of women thanking God
for their newfound freedom.)*

Thank El Shaddai for Her goodness and everlasting love!
Let all the women whom God has set free praise Her.
Let all the women whom She has rescued from oppression give thanks!

God keeps gathering them in from every land,
bringing them in from every direction.

Some wandered in the wilderness, finding no place of welcome.
Their way lay through the desert, and they found no place they belonged.
Their souls fainted with weariness.
Their hearts were hungry and thirsty for justice.
In their anguish they cried out to God, and She delivered them from distress.
She guided them to communities of welcome.
Let them thank El Shaddai for Her steadfast love,
for the wonders She has worked for women!

She satisfies the thirsting soul and fills the hungering heart with good!

Some lived in darkness, dwelling in deep shadow.
They were prisoners of suffering, chained by those who spurned justice.
Their bodies were bowed down with hard labor.
When they stumbled and fell, no one came to help them.
In their anguish they cried out to God, and She delivered them from distress.
She led them out of their darkness and gloom.
She released them from their bondage!
Let them thank El Shaddai for Her steadfast love,
for the wonders She has worked for women!

She shatters prison doors and cuts iron bars in two!

Some were sick because of their own foolishness.
They were afflicted by their own weakness.
Because they hated to eat, they drove themselves close to death.
In their anguish they cried out to God, and She delivered them from distress.

She healed them with Her word of love.
She delivered them from their self-destruction.
Let them thank El Shaddai for Her steadfast love,
for the wonders She has worked for women!

Where those who live in the land are greedy and unjust,
She makes rivers run dry, watersprings fail, fruitful land a desert.
But where She prepares a place for the hungry and needy to dwell,
She turns the desert into pools of water and dry land into living springs.
There Her chosen sow fields, plant vineyards, and reap a rich harvest.
She blesses Her daughters abundantly, and will not let them be diminished.
When powerful men seek to hem them in,
putting them down, coercing them, causing them trouble and grief,
She pours contempt on their power,
makes them wander in trackless wastes.
But El Shaddai raises up the needy, saves them from affliction,
and increases their families like flocks.

Women of integrity see these things and are glad,
but those who oppress are rendered speechless.
Let the wise ponder these things and meditate on God's steadfast love!

Prayer of the Faithful:

O my God, I adore You in all Your beauty and perfection,
which You possess in Yourself.
I adore Your splendor, a thousand times more beautiful than the sun.
I adore Your fecundity, a thousand times more wonderful
    than that of the stars.
I adore Your life, a thousand times more pleasing
    than that of the flowers.
I adore Your activity, infinitely more active than that of fire.
I adore Your stability, infinitely more fixed and solid than that of earth.
I adore Your pervasiveness, infinitely more delicate than that of air.
I adore Your gentleness, a thousand times more peaceful
    than that of our rivers.
I adore Your expanse, a thousand times more vast than that
    of the ocean. . . .

I adore Your height, a million times more sublime
    than the mountains I know. . . .
My God, in Your works, nothing is comparable to You!

Jean-Jacques Olier, 1608-1657

Benediction: May the blessing and beauty of God our Creator fill our hearts and
lives with rejoicing this day! Amen.

EVENING PRAYER

Opening:

Into Your hands, O God,
I commit my spirit.

Hymn Prayer:

It is good to sing Your praises and to thank You, El Shaddai,
showing forth Your lovingkindness when the morning lights the sky.
It is good when night is falling of Your faithfulness to tell,
while with sweet, melodious praises songs of adoration swell.

You have filled my heart with gladness
    through the works Your hands have wrought;
You have made my life victorious; great Your works
    and deep Your thought.
You in all our lives exalted, filling all our hearts with Light;
All injustices shall perish; sin be banished from Your sight!

But the just shall live before You, planted in Your dwelling place,
fruitful trees and ever verdant, nourished by Your boundless grace.
In Her goodness to the righteous God Her righteousness displays;
God, my rock, my strength and refuge, just and true are all Her ways.

Psalm 92, appearing in this verse form in The Psalter, 1912
(text modified by author)

Psalm 148

*(This might be the prayer of women
who love creation.)*

Alleluia!
Praise God from the depths and the heights.
Praise Her, all you angels in the heavens!
Praise Her, all you starry hosts!
Praise Her, all you skies and clouds.
Praise the name of El Shaddai!

For She creates whatever She wills.
And She establishes what She creates forever;
what She desires and decrees will never pass away.

Let all the creatures that live in the sea praise God from the deeps.
Let fire and hail, snow and frost, and stormy winds fulfill Her will.
Let them praise Her with all the mountains and hills,
    all the fruit trees and cedars.
Let all animals, creeping things, and birds on the wing praise Her.
Let all rulers and leaders and judges praise Her.
Let all the peoples of the earth praise Her!
Let children and elders, young and old, women and men
    praise Her together!
Praise the name of El Shaddai!
Let Her be exalted and adored,
for Her glory fills both heaven and earth!
She gives signs of salvation to all Her people —
let Her faithful ones praise Her!
Let Her daughters and sons, who long to live near Her heart,
praise Her, singing "Alleluia" forever!

Reading: Proverbs 9:1-6 or selection from the Appendix

Prayer: Intercession for human creativity, the arts, all artists, and the flourishing of beauty in every part of society

Benediction: May the blessing of our bountiful God be echoed in the praise of all people. Amen.

Week Four

Sunday

Worshiping God Our Savior

MORNING PRAYER

Opening:

The Dayspring has dawned upon us from on high
to give light to those who live in darkness
and to guide our feet into the way of peace.

Hymn Prayer:

O splendor of God's glory bright, from light eternal bringing light;
Thou Light of life, light's living spring, true Day, all days illumining:

Come, Holy Sun of heav'nly love, show'r down Thy radiance from above,
and to our inward hearts convey the Holy Spirit's cloudless ray.

And we the Mother's help will claim, and sing the Mother's glorious name;
Her powerful aid we will implore, that we may stand to fall no more.

Be hallowed this and ev'ry day, let trust now be our morning ray,
and faithful love our noonday light, and hope our sunset, calm and bright.

O God, with each returning morn Thy image to our hearts is borne,
O may we ever clearly see our Savior and our Friend in Thee!

Ambrose of Milan, 339-397
(text modified by author)

Psalm 66

(This might be the prayer of a woman Jewish cantor.)

Let all the earth shout with joy in honor of God!
Let all people give Her glory and praise.
Say to God,
"Your works are full of wonder!
Even Your enemies are struck by Your power!
All the earth adores You, and all people sing praises to exalt Your name!"

Come and see what El Shaddai has done.
Behold Her awesome acts among the peoples.
She made a path of dry land through the sea.
She parted the river, and Her people walked through it on foot!
We will always rejoice in Her whose reign is powerful love!

She examines all the nations, watches them with a keen eye.
Let none rebelliously exalt themselves at the expense of others.
Let all nations worship El Shaddai and ring out Her praises!

O God, You have given life to our souls,
    have given us firm footing on Your paths.
You have also tested us and refined us like silver.
Sometimes You have enmeshed us in difficulty and made our lives barren.
You have let others ride roughshod over us.
We have gone through fire and flood.
Yet You have brought us out into a spacious place.

I will go into the house of Your presence with precious offerings.
I will keep my solemn promises, made in the midst of trouble.
I will offer the incense of prayer to You,
and gratefully give You rich gifts in return for Your blessings.

All You who revere El Shaddai, come and listen,
give heed to the story of what She has done for my soul.
I cried aloud to Her with prayers of petition and praise.
If I had intended evil in my heart, She would not have heard me.
But She listened to me, attended to my pleas.
Blessed be El Shaddai, who opened Her ears to my supplication.
She has treated me with great mercy!

Psalm 78:1-7
(This might be the prayerful instruction
of a woman seminary professor.)

O my people, listen to my teaching!
Open your ears to the words I speak.
I will speak in parables and with ancient, mysterious sayings,
speak of what we have heard and known, of what our mothers have told us.
We must not hide these things from our children.
We must pass them on to the next generation.
We must tell them of all the wonders God has done.
We must praise Her strong and marvelous love!

She has made us Her witnesses among all the people.
She has given us Her wisdom,
and has commanded us to teach that wisdom to our children.
In this way the next generation will know Her,
and will pass on Her wisdom to their children's children.
Let us pray that they will all place their hope in God,
remembering Her wonderful works and always walking in Her wisdom!

Reading: Luke 24:1-12 or selection from the Appendix

Prayer: Intercession for the local church

Benediction: May the God who has delivered, led, and taught us through the generations bless us this day with hearts filled with praise and wills devoted to Her ways. Amen.

MIDDAY PRAYER

Opening:

O God, You are the strength of our life.
What have we to fear with You at our side?

Psalm 68:1-20, 30-35
(This might be the prayer of women the world over who yearn and work and pray for peace.)

In the end, God will arise and scatter the foes of Her shalom.
All those who hate Her will flee from before Her face.
She will blow them away like smoke in the wind;
She will melt the wicked like wax in the fire.

But those who love peace and justice will rejoice!
They will dance and sing with elation in God's presence!

Even now, we sing praises to Her name.
We make a path through the desert for Her coming.
We rejoice in the name of El Shaddai!
She is the Mother of orphans — indeed, of all children.
She is the Protector of widows — indeed, of all women.
She provides a home for the homeless.
She frees the bound and the confined.
She afflicts the unjust with parched souls.
Great is God in Her holiness!

She goes before us, our Guide as we walk through the wilderness.
In Her presence, the earth trembles,
the skies pour down showers of blessing.
When Her people languish, she restores them.
She Herself is the home of Her beloved ones.
In Her goodness She nourishes the needy.

God gives the word!
Great is the company of the women who proclaim Her good news:
"The generals and their armies are fleeing!
The women, victorious, divide their spoils!
Those who live in peace are protected by a Dove
whose wings are of silver, whose feathers gleam with gold!"

When El Shaddai scatters the might of the military,
the snow of peace falls on the mountains.
The mountain fortresses become places of serene beauty
in which God dwells in holiness forever!

Surrounded by hosts of thousands, God ascends to Her holy dwelling.
She takes captivity captive!
She receives rich gifts from the peoples,
even from those who have rebelled against Her shalom.

Blessed be El Shaddai, who bears our burdens day in and day out.
Surely She is our salvation!
Truly She is a God of healing and wholeness for us.
She alone enables escape from death. . . .

She who has done so much for us will continue to show Her strength!
She will scatter the people who delight in war.
Egypt and Ethiopia and all the nations will bring Her gifts,
will stretch out their hands to Her in prayer and praise.

Sing to God, all leaders of the earth!
Sing praises to El Shaddai!
She rides through the heavens on the wheeling stars!
She speaks with the thundering voice of many waters!
Ascribe to Her all power and glory.
Her majesty and love transcend the skies.
Adore God in Her sanctuary, standing before Her with awe.

El Shaddai gives strength to Her people!
She blesses Her beloved with peace!

Psalm 145

(This might be the prayer of a woman and the aged mother she cares for.)

My God and my Guide, I will exalt Your name forever!
I will bless You with praises every day.
I will sing with thanksgiving to You through all ages.
Your greatness is beyond all knowing and telling!

Generation after generation praises Your wonderful works.
I muse upon Your beauty and meditate on the glory of Your deeds.
With women who proclaim Your mercy, I declare Your great love.
People everywhere pour out their praises before You.
Remembering Your abundant goodness,
they sing songs of adoration to You.

You are gracious and compassionate, O God.
You are slow to anger and quick to love.
You are good to all, and Your womb-love enfolds the world.
All Your works praise You, El Shaddai.
All Your faithful people bless You.
They speak of the glory of Your loving reign.
They talk together of Your saving power.
They make Your grace known to their children.
They proclaim Your glory and beauty.

Your reign, O God, is an everlasting reign.
Your providence extends to all generations.
You are faithful in all Your works, gracious in all Your deeds.
You raise up those who fall and uphold those who are oppressed.
All those who look to You in trust are nourished by You in due time.
You open Your hand and satisfy the needs of all living creatures.
You are just in all Your ways and generous in all that You do.
You are always near those who faithfully call upon You.
You fulfill the desires of those who are devoted to You;
You hear their cry and save them.
You preserve all who love You but destroy all that opposes You.

My mouth will proclaim Your praise, O God,
and all flesh will bless Your holy name,
both now and through all ages to come!

Silence

Prayer of the Faithful:

May I be an enemy to no one and the friend of what abides eternally.
May I never quarrel with those nearest me,
and be reconciled quickly if I should.
May I never plot evil against others, and if anyone plot evil against me
may I escape unharmed and without the need to hurt anyone else.

May I love, seek, and attain only what is good.
May I desire happiness for all and harbor envy for none.
May I never find joy in the misfortune of one who has wronged me.
May I never wait for the rebuke of others,
but always rebuke myself until I make reparation. . . .

May I gain no victory that harms me or my opponent. . . .
May I reconcile friends who are angry with each other.
May I, insofar as I can, give all necessary help to my friends
and to all who are in need.
May I never fail a friend in trouble.
When visiting the grief-stricken,
may I be able to soften their pain with comforting words.

May I respect myself. . . .
May I always maintain control of my passions. . . .
May I habituate myself to be gentle,
and never be angry with others because of circumstances.
May I never discuss the wicked or what they have done,
but know good people, and follow in their footsteps.

Eusebius of Caesarea, c. 260–c. 339

Benediction:

May the blessing of God, whose praise fills the whole earth, fill all our lives
with praise this day and forever. Amen.

EVENING PRAYER

Opening:

I will go to my rest in peace,
for You alone, O God, make me dwell in safety.

Hymn Prayer:

Sun of my soul, Thou Savior dear, it is not night if Thou be near;
O may no earthborn cloud arise to hide Thee from Thy servant's eyes!

When the soft dews of kindly sleep my weary eyelids gently steep,
be my last thought, how sweet to rest forever on my Savior's breast.

Abide with me from morn till eve, for without Thee I cannot live;
abide with me when night is nigh, for without Thee I dare not die.

Watch by the sick, enrich the poor with blessings from Thy boundless store;
be every mourner's sleep tonight, like infant's slumbers, pure and light.

Come near and bless us when we wake,
'ere through the world our way we take,
'til in the ocean of Thy love we lose ourselves in heaven above.

John Keble, 1827

Psalm 72:1-8, 12-19

*(This might be the prayer of women on behalf
of all who hold political or economic power.)*

Give the gift of justice, O God, to everyone with power.
May all rulers and their successors rule with Your righteousness!
May all leaders and judges be fair and treat the lowly with mercy!
Let the mountains be places of peace for the people;
let the hills be places of justice.
May our leaders defend the cause of the poor.
May they save the children of the needy and crush all oppression!
May rulers revere You as long as the sun endures,
and honor You as long as the moon continues to shine!
May their rule be like rain that falls on new-mown grass.
May their reign be like showers that refresh the earth.
May justice flourish and peace abound in our days,
and until the moon is no more!

Above all, may Your just will prevail from sea to sea,
and from the rivers to the ends of the earth!
For You deliver the poor and needy, all those who cry out for help.
You have mercy on the weak and destitute and rescue the poverty-stricken.
You redeem their lives from violence and oppression,
for their well-being is precious in Your sight!
May Your reign last forever!
May precious gifts be given to You.
May prayer be continually offered to You.
May blessings be invoked upon You day and night!

May food be plentiful in the land.
May waves of grain cover the hilltops!
May there be fruit in abundance.
May our cities flourish like flowers in the meadows.
May Your name endure forever, Your praise last longer than the sun!
May everyone know themselves blessed by You,
and may all peoples call You blessed!

Blessed are You, El Shaddai, God of all people.
You alone do wondrous things!
Blessed be Your glorious name forever!
May the whole earth be filled with Your glory and beauty!
Amen and Amen!

Psalm 118

*(This might be the prayer of a woman
who has survived serious threats to her life.)*

Give thanks to El Shaddai,
for She is goodness itself!
Her love has no end!
Let all God's people say, "Her love has no end!"
Let all who serve God say, "Her love has no end!"
Let all who are devoted to God say, "Her love has no end!"

When I called out to God in my distress,
She answered me and released me from my anguish.
Because El Shaddai is for me, I have nothing to fear.
What can others do to me when God is there to help me?
I know I shall see the downfall of all who would destroy me.
I have found it better to take refuge in God
than to trust too much in human beings.
It is better to take shelter in God
than to put confidence in the powerful.

When I am hemmed in by adversity on every side,
God cuts me free.
When I am encircled by troubles like a swarm of stinging bees,
God scatters them.

When I am pushed so hard that I stumble,
God raises me up.
She is my strength and my song.
She has become my only salvation!

The tent of my soul is ringing with shouts of joy and victory!
God has worked wonders within me!
God's strong and sustaining hand has brought me to life!
I shall not die, but live, proclaiming Her marvelous deeds.
Though God has severely chastened me,
She has not handed me over to death.

The gates of God's generous goodness are open,
and I will enter them with thanksgiving!
All the just and faithful will enter by my side.
I will thank El Shaddai for answering me, for making me whole.

She takes a stone that has been rejected
and makes it the cornerstone of Her purpose!
Her transforming action is marvelous in our eyes!

Today is the day El Shaddai has made!
Be glad in it, and dance for joy,
for God has saved and prospered us!

Blessed are you who come in the name of El Shaddai!
We bless you in the presence of God, who has given us light.
We bear branches of celebration in festal procession.
We make our way to the altar of adoration.
We offer God our heartfelt thanks!
We extol Her glorious name!
We praise Her goodness, singing, "Her love has no end!"
Alleluia!

Reading: John 20:1-18 or selection from the Appendix

Prayer: Intercession for the worldwide church, especially for its unity

Benediction: May the blessing of God who has saved us from death and given us
new life remain with us through the week to come and throughout
our lives. Amen.

Monday

Hoping in God Our Future

MORNING PRAYER

Opening:

The Dayspring has dawned upon us from on high
to give light to those who live in darkness
and to guide our feet into the way of peace.

Hymn Prayer:

Hail to the brightness of our God's glad morning!
Joy to the lands that in darkness have lain!
Hushed by the accents of sorrow and mourning;
God in sweet triumph begins Her mild reign.

Lo, in the desert rich flowers are springing;
streams ever copious are gliding along;
loud from the mountaintops echoes are ringing;
wastes rise in verdure and mingle in song.

Hear, from all lands, from the isles of the ocean,
praise to our Savior ascending on high;
fallen the engines of war and commotion;
shouts of salvation are rending the sky!

Thomas Hastings, 1832
(text modified by author)

Psalm 46

(This might be the prayer of women in response to the daily world news.)

Our refuge and strength is in God alone,
our proven Helper in times of trouble.
Therefore we will not be afraid,
even in the face of great change.

When the mountains sink into the sea,
when ocean waters rage and foam,
when the earth is shaken by tidal waves —
still we will not be afraid.

For the river of God's peace flows through us,
a stream that makes our souls glad.
Because God makes Her home in our hearts,
we will not be shaken.
God's love dawns on us each day!

Though the nations rage at each other
while their leaders are shaken with dismay,
we know that God is with us.
The God of our mothers is our refuge.

Come and see how El Shaddai works!
She brings arrogance to ruin.
She makes wars cease all over the world.
She shatters planes and scatters missiles.
She burns tanks with Her holy fire.

Listen to the voice of God,
a voice so powerful that it melts mountains:
"Be still and know that I am God.
All the nations and all the earth will exalt Me!"

The God of the starry hosts is with us!
The God of our grandmothers is our refuge!

Psalm 81
(This might be the prayer of women seeking
to worship God in ways fitting for them.)

The God of our grandmothers is the God of our strength!
Sing aloud to Her and shout for joy!
Make sweet songs and sounds with voices and musical instruments.
Blow the trumpet to signal sweet feasting when the moon is new.
Sound the ram's horn for the full moon festival.
For this is a custom ordained by the God of our mothers!
It is the celebration of our freedom from bondage.

El Shaddai removes heavy burdens from our shoulders.
She frees our hands from forced labor.
She rescues us from our oppression.
She speaks to us in the thundering clouds.
She tests us when we drink the waters of bitterness.
She admonishes us, Her daughters, to listen only to Her.
She warns us not to worship alien gods,
to bow down to oppressive powers.

El Shaddai is our Savior and Liberator.
She promises to fill our mouths with Her goodness.
She asks us to listen carefully to Her voice.
She pleads with us not to ignore Her Spirit.
She warns us of the danger of stubbornness,
the peril of placing our wisdom above Hers.
She wants us to listen to Her,
so that She can lead us in Her ways.
She promises to subdue those who make our lives hard.
She turns Her hand against those who would hurt us.
She makes them cringe in fear and suffer the fate they deserve.
She feeds us with the finest of wheat.
She satisfies us with honey from the rock!

Reading: 1 Corinthians 12:1-13 or selection from the Appendix

Prayer: Intercession for members of the immediate family

Benediction: May the blessing of the God who frees the oppressed fill our hearts
with hope and satisfy us with the sweetness of Her presence. Amen.

MIDDAY PRAYER

Opening:

O God, You are the strength of our life.
What have we to fear with You at our side?

Psalm 75
(This might be the prayer of women working for world peace.)

When we offer You our thanks, O God, we find that You are near!
Your wonderful works make us confident that You are a fair Judge.
At the appointed time, You will rule all people with justice.
When everything seems to be falling apart,
You will steady the pillars of the earth.

The proud should not boast nor the wicked exalt themselves.
The unjust should not be high and mighty.
The powerful should not refuse to bow and yield.
They should not expect glory from any earthly quarter,
for El Shaddai alone is Judge.
She is the one who brings some low and lifts up others.
When She pours out Her wrath,
it is like a cup of foaming wine,
and the wicked must drain it to its dregs.

But we will proclaim God's glory forever.
We will sing praises to the God of our grandmothers.
For She will cut off the wicked
and exalt all those who do justice.

Psalm 98
(This might be the prayer of a women's choir.)

Sing new songs to El Shaddai for the wonders She has done!
Her helping hand and holy arm have become our health and salvation.
She has revealed Her saving purposes to all the nations.
She has been merciful and faithful to all Her people.
Her salvation has been revealed to the ends of the earth.

Let the earth cry out with joy to our God!
Let all people break out in songs of praise and dance together for joy!
Let us make sweet melodies ring out with musical instruments!
Let us make a joyful noise before Her with sounds and shouts of praise!
Let the waves of the sea roar their adoration!
Let the creatures of the ocean chorus give glory to God!
Let the rivers clap and sing with jubilation!
Let the mountains lift up their heads with exaltation!
For She is coming, coming to judge the earth.
She will judge the world with mercy and justice,
and treat all people with fairness!

Prayer of the Faithful:

O God, holy and incomprehensible, You bid light to shine out of darkness.
You have raised us up to glorify You and petition Your goodness.
Receive us who now worship You and render You what thanks we can.
Grant all our requests that will advance our salvation.
Make us children of light and day and heirs of Your eternal good things.

O God, in Your great mercy, be mindful of all here present praying with us,
as well as all our sisters and brothers in need of Your love and help —
on land, at sea, and in all places of Your dominion —
and grant them Your great mercy.
Thus, saved in soul and body, we may use the free speech of friends
to glory forever in Your wondrous and blessed Name.

Byzantine liturgy

Benediction: May the blessing of God, the Judge of all the earth, fill us with hope
in the promise of Her reign of justice and love in all places. Amen.

EVENING PRAYER

Opening:

I will go to my rest in peace,
for You alone, O God, make me dwell in safety.

Hymn Prayer:

All my hope on God is founded; She doth still my trust renew.
Me through change and chance She guideth, only good and only true.
God unknown, She alone calls my heart to be Her own.

Human pride and earthly glory, sword and crown betray Her trust.
What with care and toil we fashion, tower and temple, fall to dust.
But God's power, hour by hour, is my temple and my tower.

God's great goodness aye endureth; deep Her wisdom, passing thought.
Splendor, light, and life attend Her; beauty springeth out of nought.
Evermore from Her store newborn worlds rise and adore!

Daily doth the loving Giver bounteous gifts on us bestow;
Her desire our soul delighteth; pleasure leads us where we go.
Love doth stand at Her hand; joy doth wait on Her command!

Robert Seymour Bridges, 1844-1930
(text modified by author)

Psalm 73
(This might be the prayer of a poor, single mother.)

Those who are pure in heart find that God is good!

As for me, I nearly slipped and stumbled.
I was jealous of the power of the proud.
I resented the prosperity of the wicked.
I saw that they rarely seemed to suffer.
They looked fat, well-fed, prosperous.
They seemed exempt from troubles like mine.

I saw the jewelry they wore in their pride.
I noticed the rich clothes in which they strutted about.
Though they looked like fools to me,
I envied them their abundance.

I observed that they cared nothing for the poor.
I heard them speak with malice,
uttering cruel threats from the heights of their power.
They spoke against heaven's just demands,
yielded their tongues to lies and obscenities.
But people followed and fawned over them just the same.
They seemed to care nothing for God.
They acted as if God knows nothing!

I said to myself,
"Why are the wicked always at ease, getting richer every day?
I have kept my heart pure and my hands clean —
but have I been righteous for nothing?
Why do I suffer trouble day after day?
Why am I chastened with hardship every night?"

What I saw and thought I knew was so painful to me!
I did not want to betray the company of God's children.
But how could I grasp such apparent inequity?
The task tried my heart.

Then, as I prayed in God's holy presence, the truth finally dawned on me!
I saw that God had set the wicked on a slippery road,
that sooner or later they would slip and fall.
In the end they will be destroyed,
swept away by terror, in an instant.
The unjust are like the phantoms of dreams:
they vanish in the dawn of God's justice.

When I let my heart become bitter and cherished my pain,
I was foolish and ignorant — no better than a beast without a soul!
Yet through it all God held my hand, guiding me with Her counsel.
In the end She will bring me to glory!

O God, You are heaven to me!
I desire nothing on earth as much as I desire You!
Though my body wastes away and my heart faints and fails,
You are the rock of my soul!
You are the treasure of my heart!
I will cherish You forever!

I see that those who wander far from Your ways will suffer,
that those who betray You will be cut off.
As for me, to be near You is my greatest good.
You are my refuge, and I will praise You for all that You do!

Psalm 113

*(This might be the prayer of a woman living in a shelter
for homeless women and their children.)*

Alleluia!
Adore El Shaddai for all that She is!
Serve Her with praise and thanksgiving!
Bless Her name both now and forever!
Praise Her from the rising to the setting of the sun!

El Shaddai is exalted among all peoples.
Her glory fills the heavens, lights up the skies.
She is great beyond all thought, majestic beyond comparison.
There is no one else like El Shaddai!
She who is so great bends low in love to the earth She has made.
She raises poor women from the dust, rescues children from the streets.
She places them among the powerful, the leaders of Her people.
She gives despised women a home and makes them joyful mothers.
Alleluia!

Reading: Ephesians 4:1-16 or selection from the Appendix

Prayer: Intercession for the extended family

Benediction: May the name of our God be blessed in all the earth, and may Her blessing rest upon all the poor and needy and fill their hearts and ours with hope. Amen.

Tuesday

Seeking God's Wisdom

MORNING PRAYER

Opening:

The Dayspring has dawned upon us from on high
to give light to those who live in darkness
and to guide our feet into the way of peace.

Hymn Prayer:

O Come, Thou Dayspring, come and cheer our spirits by Thine advent here;
disperse the gloomy clouds of night, and death's dark shadows put to flight.
Rejoice! Rejoice! Immanuel shall come to thee, O Israel!

O Come, Desire of nations, bind all peoples in one heart and mind:
bid Thou our sad divisions cease; fill the whole world with heaven's peace.
Rejoice! Rejoice! Immanuel shall come to thee, O Israel!

O come, Thou Wisdom from on high, Who ord'rest all things mightily;
to us the path of knowledge show and teach us in her ways to go.
Rejoice! Rejoice! Immanuel shall come to thee, O Israel!

Medieval antiphons

Psalm 119:137-52
(This might be the prayer of a woman student
at a public university.)

El Shaddai, You are always generous and just.
All that You say is truthful and right.
When people forget Your Word, zeal for Your truth burns within me.
Your Word is pure, rich with promises, and I love it.
Though very few people listen to me, I do not forget Your precepts.
I find truth in Your ways and goodness in Your commands.
When I am distressed, I delight myself in Your Word.
I know that Your precepts are forever true;
help me understand how to live by them faithfully.
With my whole heart I cry to You for help in keeping Your laws.
Before the day dawns I wait for Your wisdom in hope.
I stay awake far into the night to meditate on Your Word.

Hear me in Your mercy, El Shaddai, and in justice give me abundant life.
When doubts and difficulties tempt me to spurn Your ways,
be near me, O God, and keep me true to Your will.
I seek to understand Your designs through the ages.
I know Your purposes are firmly founded and last forever.

Reading: Acts 18:24-28 or selection from the Appendix

Prayer: Intercession for friends and neighbors

Benediction: May the blessing of God's will guide our footsteps throughout this
day and bring light to our entire lives. Amen.

MIDDAY PRAYER

Opening:

O God, You are the strength of our life.
What have we to fear with You at our side?

Psalm 119:153-76

(This might be the prayer of a woman experiencing spiritual trials.)

When I am greatly afflicted within, O God, make speed to save me!
Help me to remember Your life-giving Word.
Deliver and defend me with Your Spirit.
Those who do not seek Your will are far from salvation and wholeness.
Yet Your lovingkindness is great, El Shaddai.
In Your justice and mercy grant me life eternal.
My soul has many enemies, yet I struggle to follow Your paths.
I am grieved by the treachery in my heart,
which makes me resist Your directions.
Yet I love Your precepts, O God, for they renew my life.
All Your words are forever true, all Your judgments just.

I find myself persecuted by powerful forces around me,
so I devote my heart to Your Word.
I rejoice in Your wisdom like one who finds great treasure.
I love Your truth and wisdom, but despise my self-deception.
Seven times a day I praise You for all Your generous judgments.
Those who love Your will are blessed with great peace.
They do not stumble over the obstacles in their path.
I share their hope for Your deliverance, El Shaddai.
With them I try to obey Your commands.
My soul attends to Your voice, lingering on Your words,
and I try to follow Your will.
All my ways are open to You!

Hear my cry, El Shaddai!
Give me wisdom through Your Word.
Honor my prayer for deliverance as You have promised.
When You teach me Your ways, my lips will sing Your praises!
Your Word will be on my tongue, Your wise commands in my heart.
Lend me a helping hand, for I have chosen to follow Your ways.
I long for the wholeness that only You can give, El Shaddai!
I will make Your desires my delight;
I will praise You for giving new life to my soul;
I will trust in Your mercy to help me.
Like a lost child I have wandered away from You.
Seek me out as I cling to Your Word.

Prayer of the Faithful:

Holy Spirit, Your fiery Love warms the whole earth.
Your Beauty blazes into sun and fire.
You radiate Glory within and without.
The flame of Your womanly Wisdom burns in the shrine of my soul.
The heat of Your Compassion melts my cold heart,
and penetrates my whole body's being.
I rest in Your radiance, and respond to Your calling,
filled with the Light of Your Divine Presence. Amen.

Anonymous, 20th century

Benediction: May the God who is always more ready to give than we are to receive open our hearts to receive the blessing of Her wisdom and nurture in this day and always. Amen.

EVENING PRAYER

Opening:

I will go to my rest in peace,
for You alone, O God, make me dwell in safety.

Hymn Prayer:

Open my eyes, that I may see glimpses of truth Thou hast for me;
place in my hands the wonderful key that shall unclasp and set me free.
Silently now I wait for Thee; ready, my God, Thy will to see.
Open my eyes, illumine me, Spirit Divine!

Open my ears, that I may hear voices of truth Thou sendest clear;
and while the wavenotes fall on my ear, everything false will disappear.
Silently now I wait for Thee; ready, my God, Thy will to see.
Open my ears, illumine me, Spirit Divine!

Open my mouth, and let me bear gladly the warm truth everywhere;
open my heart and let me prepare love with Thy children thus to share.
Silently now I wait for Thee; ready, my God, Thy will to see.
Open my heart, illumine me, Spirit Divine!

Clara Scott, 1895

Psalm 127
(This might be the musing of a midwife.)

> If God does not build the house, its builders labor for nothing.
> If God does not keep the city, its protectors guard it in vain.
> It is useless to rise up early and stay up late,
> eating the bread of anxious toil.
> God gives Her beloved peaceful sleep!
>
> Daughters are a heritage from God.
> The fruit of the womb is Her reward.
> Like threads of colored silk in the hand of a weaver,
> so are the daughters of one's youth!
> Happy is the woman who has a hand full of them!
> She shall not be ashamed when critics confront her!

Psalm 128
*(This might be the blessing of a mother
on the occasion of her daughter's wedding.)*

> If you devote yourself to El Shaddai, great blessing will rest upon you!
> If you faithfully walk in Her good ways, great blessing will fall upon you!
>
> You will surely enjoy the fruit of your labor.
> You will grow in happiness and enjoy well-being.
> Your husband will be like a fruitful seed in your garden.
> Your children will flower in beauty around your table.
> Receive the blessing of El Shaddai, my devoted daughter!
> May God bless you with holy living.
> May you prosper with all God's people as long as you live!
> May you live to see your great-grandchildren!
> Peace be upon you and your household!
> Peace be upon all of God's household!

Reading: Acts 21:7-9 or selection from the Appendix

Prayer: Intercession for adversaries/enemies/competitors

Benediction: May the blessing of God make you fruitful in all your works and ways, and grant you restful sleep through the night. Amen.

Wednesday

Trusting in God Our Refuge

MORNING PRAYER

Opening:

> The Dayspring has dawned upon us from on high
> to give light to those who live in darkness
> and to guide our feet into the way of peace.

Hymn Prayer:

> Forth in Thy Name, O God, I go, my daily labor to pursue;
> Thee, only Thee, resolved to know, in all I think or speak or do.
>
> The task Thy wisdom hath assigned O let me cheerfully fulfill;
> in all my works Thy Presence find, and prove Thy good and perfect will.
>
> Thee may I set at my right hand, whose eyes my inmost substance see,
> and labor on at Thy command, and offer all my works to Thee.

Charles Wesley, 1749

Psalm 62

*(This might be the prayer of a Latin American woman
protesting oppression by the rich and powerful.)*

My soul silently waits for God's salvation.
She alone is my rock and my refuge.
She is a tower of strength for me.
She makes me whole and keeps me from being shaken.

How long will all of you attack the poor,
trying to topple their weak defenses?
How long will you plot to bring them down?
How long will you take pleasure in falsehood?
How long will your mouths be filled with compliments
while your hearts are full of curses?

The poor and powerless wait silently for God.
She alone gives them hope.
She is their rock and their refuge,
their tower of strength and salvation.
In Her they will never be shaken.

Our freedom and dignity rest with God, in whom we find refuge.
She is a strong rock of defense for us.
Trust in Her at all times, my sisters.
Pour out your hearts before Her, all you poor and powerless.
God is surely our protector!

Those who are rich and powerful are deluded.
They imagine themselves to be important,
but they weigh less than a breath in the balance of God's justice!
It is foolish for them to trust in oppression.
It is folly for them to place their hope in cheating schemes.

Let no one set their hearts on increasing riches!
For God has spoken again and again,
reminding us that all true power belongs to Her alone.
In justice and love She will reward us according to our deeds.

Psalm 90

*(This might be the prayer of aged women
living alone or in nursing homes.)*

El Shaddai, You have been our home in every generation!
Before You gave birth to the earth or the mountains came to be,
You were and are and are to come — God without beginning or end.
You made us children of earth, and we return to its dust.
In Your eyes, a thousand years ago is like yesterday to us.
The ages pass as swiftly for You as nights do for us.
Our lives are like dreams, dreams that slip away when we awake.
We bloom, like flowers, for a day.
Fresh in the morning, we wither and die in the evening.

We are devastated at the prospect of Your anger.
Our guilt is exposed, our secret sins revealed by the light of Your face.
Our days and years are little more than swiftly fleeting sighs.
Our human span is seventy years — eighty for those who are strong.
How quickly those years pass,
years filled with toil and trouble!
Like migrating birds, we fly through the sky of life — and are gone.

Who among us truly realizes the purifying power of your loving anger?
Who genuinely reveres You for Your righteous wrath against evil?
Teach us to see how short our lives are,
so that our hearts might grow wise.

When will You turn to us, O God, and have mercy on those who serve You?
Fill us with Your love at the dawn of each new day.
Then we will be able to rejoice as long as we live.
Balance the griefs of our lives with gladness!
Let us see good for as long as we have seen evil.
Reveal the mystery of Your designs to us, Your daughters.
Let Your beauty and love become plain to our children.
Let Your favor rest upon us, El Shaddai!
Prosper the work of our lives, that it might bear fruit in the future.

Reading: Matthew 25:1-13 or selection from the Appendix

Prayer: Intercession for the local community, town, or city

Benediction: May God bless us with love which overwhelms all hurt and anger, and grace which establishes all our good work. Amen.

MIDDAY PRAYER

Opening:

O God, You are the strength of our life.
What have we to fear with You at our side?

Psalm 121
(This might be the prayer of a woman for her children
or friends before they leave on a journey.)

I raise my eyes to the hills, looking for help and protection.
Our help comes from El Shaddai, Mother of heaven and earth!

She is the mighty, breasted God of the mountains.
She will not let your feet slip as you journey along.
She will watch and keep you with unsleeping eye.
She who watches Her children never slumbers!

El Shaddai is Your shelter and shade.
You have nothing to fear in the brightness of the sun,
nor in the light of the moon.
El Shaddai will guard you from evil.
She will preserve your soul and protect your life.
El Shaddai will always be with you as you come and go,
both now and forever. Amen.

Psalm 125

(This might be the prayer of a woman pastor
opening a service of praise.)

You who trust in El Shaddai will be as immoveable as mountains!
You will abide in Her holy presence forever!

El Shaddai surrounds Her people with protection,
like the everlasting mountains
that surround the Holy City.
She will remove all corruption and injustice,
purifying the places where Her people dwell.
She will keep Her people from turning their hands to wrong.
She will be good to those who are good,
to the just and generous of heart.
But those who insist on their own crooked ways will be abandoned,
will be left in the lurch with other evildoers.

May God's peace dwell among all Her people!

Prayer of the Faithful:

O God, I do not know what to ask of You.
You alone know my real needs,
and You love me more than I even know how to love.
Enable me to discern my true needs which are hidden from me.
I ask for neither a cross nor a consolation,
but simply wait in patience for You.
My heart is open to You.

For Your great mercy's sake, come to me and help me.
Put Your mark on me and heal me, cast me down and raise me up.
I silently adore Your holy will and Your mysterious ways.
I offer myself in sacrifice to You and put all my trust in You alone.
I desire only to do Your will.
Teach me how to pray, and pray in me Yourself.

Vasily Drozdov Philaret, Russian Orthodox, 1782-1867

Benediction: May the blessings of God we have experienced throughout our lives enable us now to trust in Her continued blessing, in which She gives us life and power and enables us to flourish and be fruitful. Amen.

EVENING PRAYER

Opening:

I will go to my rest in peace,
for You alone, O God, make me dwell in safety.

Hymn Prayer:

Now on land and sea descending, brings the night its peace profound;
Let our vesper hymn be blending with the holy calm around.
Jubilate! Jubilate! Jubilate, amen.

Soon as dies the sunset glory, stars of heaven shine out above,
telling still the ancient story, their Creator's changeless love.
Jubilate! Jubilate! Jubilate, amen.

Now our wants and burdens leaving to God's care, Who cares for all,
cease we fearing, cease we grieving, touched by Her, our burdens fall.
Jubilate! Jubilate! Jubilate, amen.

As the darkness deepens o'er us, lo! eternal stars arise;
hope and faith and love rise glorious, shining in the Spirit's skies.
Jubilate! Jubilate! Jubilate, amen.

Samuel Longfellow, 1859
(text modified by author)

Psalm 91

(This might be a prayer for women worried for their safety.)

You who shelter in the shadow of El Shaddai's wings
shall abide in the secret place of God's presence.
You will say to El Shaddai,
"You are my refuge and the home of my heart.
You are my God, and I trust in You."
She will keep you from falling into traps.
She will deliver you from plagues of destruction.
She will cover you with Her wings and gather you to Her breast.
Her faithful love will surround you with protection.

You need not fear the terror that stalks in the night,
nor the threats aimed at you during the day,
nor the evil that lurks in the darkness,
nor the destruction that strikes in broad daylight.
Though thousands fall into evil around you, evil shall not come near you.

You shall see the violent reap their just reward.
But you, who have made the Holy One your habitation,
shall find in Her the refuge you need.
No evil will befall your soul, no plague come near your dwelling.
El Shaddai will order Her angels to guard you in all that you do.
They will hold you by the hand and keep you from stumbling into danger.
You will tread underfoot all that threatens to harm you.

Because you cling to God in loving trust, She will surely deliver you.
She knows your name and understands your heart.
She will protect you and be with you in every kind of trouble.
When you call to Her, She will answer you in love.
She will clothe you with dignity and help you walk in freedom.
She will satisfy you with long life.
You will see the fullness of Her saving power!

Psalm 124

*(This might be the prayer of women everywhere in their
increasingly successful struggle for dignity and freedom.)*

If El Shaddai had not been on our side,
had not held us up when so many men tried to keep us down,
we would have been swallowed alive in the flood of their anger.
The waves of their oppression would have swept us away.
The torrents of their resistance would have overwhelmed us.
We would have drowned in the raging waters of their opposition.

Blessed be El Shaddai, who has *not* given us over to them as helpless prey!
We have escaped from their snares like birds from the hunter!
Their traps have been opened, and we have flown away free!

Our help is in the name of El Shaddai, mother of heaven and earth!

Reading: Matthew 15:21-28 or selection from the Appendix

Prayer: Intercession for the larger community, state, province, etc.

Benediction: May the God in whom we can always find refuge bless everyone in
danger this night from every kind of evil, and grant us all Her peace.
Amen.

Thursday

Crying Out to God for Justice

MORNING PRAYER

Opening:

The Dayspring has dawned upon us from on high
to give light to those who live in darkness
and to guide our feet into the way of peace.

Hymn Prayer:

As the sun doth daily rise, brightening up the eastern skies,
so to Thee with one accord open we our hearts, O God.

Day by day provide us food, for from Thee come all things good;
strength unto our souls afford from Thy living Bread, O God.

Be our guard in sin and strife; be the leader of our life;
lest from Thee we stray abroad, stay our wayward feet, O God.

Latin hymn, translated by J. Masters
and adapted by Horatio Nelson, 1864

Psalm 58

*(This might be the prayer of women fighting
violent tyranny wherever it is found.)*

Do you really decree what is right, you who rule our nations?
Do you treat women and their daughters with justice?
Indeed not!
In your hearts you devise wrongdoing,
and your hands inflict injury and violence.
From the beginning you have ruled wickedly.
From the start you have strayed from God's path.
Your ways are as venomous as poisonous snakes!
No amount of skillful speaking can get you to listen.
You resist the pleas of the wisest and best who call you to change.
You hear no better than a deaf adder!

But God will break the force of your threats.
She will remove your poisonous fangs!
She will decimate your weapons and destroy your harmful power.
Your plans will dissolve like dirt in water!
Your tyrannous trails, like the snail's, will melt into slime!
Your mischief-making will miscarry; your plots will be aborted.
God will sweep you away with the whirlwind of Her wrath.
As quickly as pots feel the heat of the fire, you will feel the flames of Her anger!

But we who try to live with integrity will rejoice in the vengeance of God!
We will all benefit from the downfall of your wickedness.
We will see that there is surely a reward for the righteous.

Do not forget that there is a just God who judges all the earth!

Psalm 59

(This might be the prayer of a woman threatened by organized crime.)

O God, deliver me from my enemies!
People in high places rise against me,
people who are evil and bloodthirsty.
They band together and lie in wait for me.
Save my life from their attacks, I beg You!

I am not guilty of any wrongdoing,
yet they are prepared to destroy me.

Awaken to my peril, El Shaddai!
Arise to punish the violent,
and do not spare the treacherous.

Every night they growl their threats,
roaming the streets like wild dogs.
They bark curses and snarl obscenities at me.
They do not care who hears them.

But You, El Shaddai, shall laugh at them.
You shall mock them and their kind.
In confidence I keep watch, waiting for Your help.
You are my strength and my stronghold.
You will save me with Your steadfast love.

Let me someday witness the downfall of my foes.
Do not let people forget their terrible deeds.
Scatter them by Your strength, O God.
Bring them to justice and destroy their power!
Trap them in their own pride and arrogance.
Consume the curses and lies of their sinful mouths.
Take them away from among us.

Let everyone see that You protect Your faithful ones everywhere.
Then I will sing loudly of Your saving power.
I will praise Your mercy every morning,
naming You my strong defense, my refuge in days of distress.
I will offer You my thanks, O my Strength!
You are my stronghold of steadfast love and protection.

Reading: Mark 12:18-27 or selection from the Appendix

Prayer: Intercession for one's own country and its leaders

Benediction: May the God of justice and shalom bless us and the world with these
gifts, and may we become more ready to receive them. Amen.

MIDDAY PRAYER

Opening:

O God, You are the strength of our life.
What have we to fear with You at our side?

Psalm 64
(This might be a woman's plea for help in trouble.)

O God, hear my complaints!
Guard my life from dread and fear.
Protect me from corruption and chaos,
and hide me from those who do evil.
Defend me from tongues sharp as knives;
shield me from hateful words that fly like bullets around me.
Keep me from being ambushed by my enemies.
Rescue me from the snares of evil.
Let those who cunningly conceive injustice be warned.
Let them realize that You are watching!

How deep and dark are the inner workings of human hearts!

But You will suddenly wound what is wicked.
You will shoot down evil plots,
will bring Your enemies to ruin.
Their wicked words will recoil on their own heads.

All who see their ruin will be shaken.
People will revere Your deeds and declare Your saving acts.
The upright will rejoice in You and ponder the results of Your justice.
The just will take refuge in You,
and those with integrity of heart will glory in Your name!

Prayer of the Faithful:

O God, by all your dealings with us,
whether of joy or pain, of light or darkness,
let us be brought to You.
Let us value no treatment of Your grace
simply because it makes us happy or because it makes us sad,
or because it gives us or denies us what we want.

But may all that You send us bring us to You,
that knowing Your perfect goodness,
we may be sure in every disappointment that You are still loving us,
and in every darkness that You are still enlightening us,
and in every enforced idleness that You are still using us,
yes, in every death that You are giving us Life.

Phillips Brooks, 1835-1893

Benediction: May God the Righteous Judge, Loving Protector, and Tender Healer
bless us and all people this day with justice, protection, and healing,
according to our needs. Amen.

EVENING PRAYER

Opening:

I will go to my rest in peace,
for You alone, O God, make me dwell in safety.

Hymn Prayer:

O Loving God, most earnestly I seek Your holy face,
within Your dwelling place to see the glories of Your grace.
Apart from You I long and thirst, and naught can satisfy;
I wander in a desert land where all the streams run dry.

The lovingkindness of my God is more than life to me,
so I will praise Her all my days and pray continually.
In Her my soul is satisfied, my darkness turns to light,
and joyful meditations fill the watches of the night.

Beneath the shadow of Your wings I sing my joy and praise.
Your right hand is my strong support through troubled nights and days.
All evil threats against my soul will fail at Your command.
With all Your people, I will trust my life into Your hand.

Psalm 63, appearing in this verse form in *The Psalter,* 1912
(text modified by author)

Psalm 70

(This might be the prayer of a woman suffering sexual harassment.)

O God, hurry to help me!
Deliver me from those who seek to injure me!
Confuse and confound them for my sake.
Turn back those who would hurt me.
Humiliate those who seek to humiliate me.
Embarrass those who seek to embarrass me.

Let me be glad and rejoice in You with all those who love Your will.
May all of us who experience Your salvation constantly praise Your Name.

O God, come quickly to my aid, for I am needy and vulnerable.
Deliver me, El Shaddai, with no further delay!

Psalm 71

*(This might be the prayer of an aged woman living
in a dangerous neighborhood.)*

When I take refuge in You, O God, do not let me down!
In Your justice rescue me from harm.
Listen to me and save me when I am threatened.
Be for me my rock, my strength of protection.
Deliver me from the hands of the wicked, O God.
Save me from the power of the ruthless.

You have given me Your Word as my defense.
You, El Shaddai, are my only hope.
Since I was a child I have trusted in You.
Since birth I leaned on Your everlasting arms.
You delivered me from my mother's womb.
I will always praise You!

Because You have been my constant refuge and strength,
I have been a sign of Your saving power for many.
My mouth is filled with songs of Your glory all the day long.

Now that I am old, do not cast me away!
Do not forsake me now that my strength fails.
Hostile people live around me, watching my every move.
They plot and scheme together to harm me.
"God has left her," they say. "Pursue and seize her.
She has no one to help her."
O God, do not be far from me.
Come quickly to my rescue, El Shaddai!
Shame those who would put me to shame.
Let those who would hurt me be heaped with disgrace!

As for me, I will hope in You always.
I will praise You more and more without ceasing.
I will speak of Your just deeds and saving acts all the day long,
though their number is beyond all telling.
I will come and go in Your strength alone, El Shaddai.
I will declare Your generous goodness.

O God, You have been my teacher since I was a youth.
To this day I sing of Your wonders.
Now that I am old and gray, do not forsake me.
I want to declare Your salvation to the coming generation,
for Your power and justice are as great as the heavens.
You are an incomparable God who has done marvelous things.
Though You have let me see trouble and evil multiply,
You have always revived me again.
I know You will continue to grant me well-being,
will fill me with comfort and calm. . . .

I will praise You in song for Your constant kindness!
I will sing with thanksgiving to You, O Holy One of Blessing!
I will shout for joy, for You always rescue my soul.
I will talk of Your goodness each day,
for You have reached out and saved me,
have shamed those who sought to harm me.

Reading: Mark 12:41-44 or selection from the Appendix

Prayer: Intercession for the welfare of other countries and for wisdom for their leaders

Benediction: May the blessing of the God of all ages be with us in youth and old age and fill our mouths with the praise of Her goodness. Amen.

Friday

Confession and Lamentation before God

MORNING PRAYER

Opening:

> The Dayspring has dawned upon us from on high
> to give light to those who live in darkness
> and to guide our feet into the way of peace.

Hymn Prayer:

> Nobody knows the trouble I see;
> nobody knows my sorrow.
> Nobody knows the trouble I see —
> glory, hallelujah!
>
> Sometimes I'm up; sometimes I'm down —
> O yes, Lord.
> Sometimes I'm almost to the ground —
> O yes, Lord.
>
> Although you see me going 'long so —
> O yes, Lord.
> I have my trials here below —
> O yes, Lord.

Nobody knows the trouble I see;
nobody knows my sorrow.
Nobody knows the trouble I see —
glory, hallelujah!

Afro-American spiritual

Psalm 42
*(This might be the prayer of a woman mourning
her alienation from the church.)*

Like a deer panting with thirst for flowing streams,
my soul pants with longing for You, El Shaddai.
My heart thirsts for the true and living God.
When will I be able to see Her face?
My tears flow both day and night
while others question the God I seek.

Memories pour forth from my soul:
I remember how I used to lead people in processions of praise,
singing glad songs of worship and celebrating the great feasts.

Why are you cast down and groaning within me, my soul?
I will hope in El Shaddai, who has always been at my side.
There will come a time when I can publicly thank Her!
But now I feel distant from the God of my tradition.
I sink into sadness, awash in waves of grief.
Great sorrow floods the depths of my heart.

Yet each day I experience the kindness of El Shaddai,
and each night I sing songs to Her in my heart.
I pray constantly to the God who gives me life.

I wonder why God sometimes seems to have forgotten us.
I wonder why we still go mourning because of our oppression.
The taunts of those who oppose us are like deadly wounds in our souls.
They are constantly questioning our desire to worship God in our way.
"What and where is this God of yours?" they derisively say.

Why sink so low, moaning in pain within me, my soul?
Hope in El Shaddai, for I will continue to thank Her,
my God, my heart's desire, and my help.

Psalm 88:13-18
(This might be the prayer of a young woman with cancer.)

In the morning I cry out in prayer to You, El Shaddai.
Why do You cast me off?
Why do You hide from me?
Though I am young, I am afflicted;
in my youth I find myself close to death!
I am overcome with fear and perplexity.
Wrath overwhelms me, and terror separates me from You.
My suffering sweeps over me like a flood.
Even my friends and my lover refuse to be close to me.
My companions cannot penetrate the darkness that surrounds me.
Come help me, my light and my life!

Reading: Matthew 27:45-61 or selection from the Appendix

Prayer: Intercession for the world and for justice and mercy for its women

Benediction: May the God of mercy, who is well acquainted with grief, bless us with gentle comfort and healing for our sorrows. Amen.

MIDDAY PRAYER

Opening:

O God, You are the strength of our life.
What have we to fear with You at our side?

Psalm 69

(This might be the prayer of a woman prophet and reformer.)

Save me from drowning in disaster, O God!
I have lost my foothold and am mired in mud.
I am sinking in deep water, overwhelmed by a flood of trouble.
Weeping has worn me out; my throat is dry with sobbing.
My eyes grow dim as I watch for Your help.

There are so many people who senselessly hate me,
more than there are hairs on my head!
The powerful seek to destroy me with lies.
Must I repent of things I have not done?

You see my folly and hidden sins, O God.
Do not let those who hope in You be let down because of me.
Do not let those who seek You be discouraged on my account.
For I am shamed and reproached for Your sake, El Shaddai!
Women who should be like sisters to me treat me like a stranger.
Men who should be brothers to me treat me as if I were an alien.

Because I am consumed by zeal for Your Word and Your holy house,
those who insult or ignore You heap insults on me.
When I fast and weep, they reprimand me!
When I go mourning, they ridicule me!
People criticize me in public, and drunkards mockingly sing of me.

Still I pray to You, El Shaddai, seeking Your loving favor.
Be faithful to me, O God, and lift me from the mire!
Deliver me from those who hate me.
Do not let this flood of opposition overwhelm me.
Do not let me drown in the depths or perish in the pit of despair.
For goodness' sake, answer me in mercy!
Embrace me in the fullness of Your womb-love.
Do not hide from me but hurry to save me!
Draw near to me and redeem me.
Free me from all my enemies, both within and without.

You know how I am shamed and reproached.
You see how I am dishonored.
You know who my enemies are.

My heart is broken and my soul is sick!
I have looked for mercy in vain.
No one offers me comfort or gives me solace.
I am poor and in pain, O God.
Save me and grant me protection.

Trap those who attack me when they least expect it.
Snare them when they think they are safe!
Darken their eyes and make them tremble!
Pour out Your indignation upon their wickedness;
let Your anger burn their sins away.
Make their hearts and homes desolate.
For they persecute those who are already stricken,
attack those already pierced with pain.
Make them feel guilty for their sins!
Let them suffer the consequences of their malice.
Blot them out from the records of Your people;
do not count them among those who are faithful to You.

I will praise and magnify You, O God.
I will sing songs of thanksgiving to You.
This will please You far more than the costliest offerings.
When the oppressed hear of it, they will rejoice.
The hearts of the humble who seek You will be revived.
For You hear the needy and help those who are in bondage.

Let heaven and earth praise You!
Let the seas and all that lives in them adore You!
For You save Your people and sustain their communities.
They shall live in peace and possess Your promises.
They shall pass on their heritage to their children.
All those who love You shall dwell safely in Your presence.

Prayer of the Faithful:

O God, teach me to see You, and reveal Yourself to me when I seek You.
For I cannot seek You unless You first teach me,
nor find You unless You first reveal Yourself to me.
Let me seek You in longing, and long for You in seeking.
Let me find You in love, and love You in finding.

Ambrose of Milan, 339-397

Too late have I loved You, O Beauty so ancient, O Beauty so new,
too late have I loved You!
You were within me but I was outside myself, and I sought You there!
In my weakness I ran after the beauty of the things You have made.
You were with me, and I was not with You.
The things You have made kept me from You —
the things which would have no being unless they existed in You!

You have called, You have cried out, and You have pierced my deafness.
You have radiated forth, and have shined out brightly,
and You have dispelled my blindness.
You have sent forth Your fragrance, and I have breathed it in,
and I long for You.
I have tasted You, and I hunger and thirst for You.
You have touched me, and I ardently desire Your peace.

Augustine of Hippo, 354-430

Benediction: May the God who listens to our hearts and enters into our pain bless
us and all who are in need with the comfort and quiet of Her gentle
presence, now and always. Amen.

EVENING PRAYER

Opening:

> I will go to my rest in peace,
> for You alone, O God, make me dwell in safety.

Hymn Prayer:

> From noon of joy to night of doubt our feelings come and go;
> our best estate is toss'd about in ceaseless ebb and flow.
> No mood of feeling, form of thought, is constant for a day,
> but Thou, O God, Thou changest not; the same Thou art always.
>
> I grasp Thy strength, make it my own, my heart with peace is bless'd;
> I lose my hold, and then comes down darkness and cold unrest.
> Let me no more my comfort draw from my frail grasp of Thee:
> in this alone rejoice with awe, Thy mighty grasp of me.
>
> Thy purpose of eternal good let me but surely know;
> on this I'll lean, let changing mood and feeling come and go;
> glad when Thy sunshine fills my soul, not sad when clouds o'er cast,
> since Thou within Thy sure control of Love dost hold me fast.

John Campbell Shairp, 1871

Psalm 74:1-11, 18-23
(This might be the prayer of women who are angry
with those who pollute and destroy the earth.)

> O God, do not cast us away for our carelessness!
> Do not let the smoke of your anger rise against us.
> You have always remembered, gathered, and cared for Your people.
> You have redeemed Your heritage.
> You are worshiped in Your holy dwelling places.
> Yet, see the ruins created by Your enemies.
> The spoilers are desecrating Your home on this earth.

They have violated Your holy sanctuaries in city and wilderness.
They have set up their own signs in place of Your Signs.
They have hacked down the ancient trees with axes,
splintered the precious wood with hatchets.
They have set fires in the places You have created.
They have polluted Your holy habitation!
They have tried to exploit the earth and all that is in it,
have tried to subdue all those who resist them.
They have destroyed the beauty in which we could meet You.

We can no longer see the signs of Your presence with clarity.
We can no longer hear the voices of those who speak for You.
We cannot tell when this destruction of creation will end.

How long, O God, will the greedy scoff at our resistance?
How long will the despoilers revile Your will?
How long will You refrain from taking action? . . .
See how the powerful blaspheme against You.
See how the impious defile Your creation.
Do not give up Your beloved to their beastly behavior.
Do not forget us in our affliction.
Remember the covenant You made with us.

The land is full of violence and the darkness of oppression.
Do not abandon those who are suffering.
Give the weak and needy glad reason to rise and praise Your name!
Arise and plead Your cause, O God!
Confront the greedy who scorn You every day.
Demand restitution for the damage Your enemies have done.
Quell the continuous uproar Your adversaries make!

Reading: Luke 3:50-56 or selection from the Appendix

Prayer: Intercession for all the world's children, and for a future of peace and well-being for them

Benediction: May the God who cares passionately for the earth and all that lives in it bless us with the same caring compassion and preserve us from greed and violence, now and always. Amen.

Saturday

Praising God the Creator

MORNING PRAYER

Opening:

The Dayspring has dawned upon us from on high
to give light to those who live in darkness
and to guide our feet into the way of peace.

Hymn Prayer:

For the beauty of the earth, for the glory of the skies,
for the love which from our birth over and around us lies,
God of all, to You we raise this, our hymn of grateful praise.

For the wonder of each hour of the day and of the night,
hill and vale and tree and flower, sun and moon and stars of light,
God of all, to You we raise this, our hymn of grateful praise.

For the joy of ear and eye, for the heart and mind's delight,
for the mystic harmony linking sense to sound and sight,
God of all, to You we raise this, our hymn of grateful praise.

For the joy of human love, sister, brother, parent, child,
friends on earth and friends above; for all gentle thoughts and mild,
God of all, to You we raise this, our hymn of grateful praise.

Folliot S. Pierpoint, 1867

215

*(This might be a prayer offered by a woman
after the birth of her first grandchild.)*

I will sing forever of God's tender mercies!
I will proclaim Her faithfulness to my children and grandchildren.
I will show that Her faithfulness is as firm as the heavens,
and that Her mercy continues to increase.

Let the skies join me in proclaiming Your praise, O God!
Let the assemblies of the chosen sing of Your faithfulness.
No other power in heaven or earth compares with You!
None among the mighty are like You in power!
The company of the faithful greatly reveres You;
the hosts who surround You stand in awe.
No being is as great as You are!

In Your greatness You rule the pride of the sea.
When its waves rise high, You still them.
You crush monstrous chaos and scatter Your foes.
Heaven and earth belong to You:
the world and all its bounty is Yours.
Because You created all things,
they owe their existence to You.

The towering mountains shout Your name with joy.
Your arm is mighty to save, Your hand filled with strength.
The foundations of Your reign are justice and generosity.
Mercy and truth shine from Your face.

Blessed are the people who know how to celebrate You!
Blessed are those who live in the light of Your presence,
who rejoice in You every day and take delight in Your goodness.
You are their glory and their strength.
You exalt them with Your favor.

Reading: Wisdom 7:22-28 (Apocrypha) or selection from the Appendix

Prayer: Intercession for all creation — the environment, all creatures, and the earth

Benediction: May the blessing of God our Mother and Father, Redeemer and Friend, Comforter and Advocate fill your life with joy this day and forever. Amen.

MIDDAY PRAYER

Opening:

O God, You are the strength of our life.
What have we to fear with You at our side?

Psalm 114
(This might be the prayer of a woman rabbi.)

When our grandmothers came out of bondage,
the house of Sarah from an alien people,
they became the sanctuary of God,
the domain of El Shaddai.

When the seas saw this, they parted and fled.
The rivers turned back.
The mountains skipped like restless rams.

Why did the seas flee?
Why did the rivers turn back?
Why did the mountains skip like rams?

Because all the earth trembles at Her presence,
the presence of El Shaddai, the God of Sarah!
She turns rocks into pools of water, flint into bubbling springs!

Psalm 149

(This might be the prayer of women liturgical dancers.)

Alleluia!
Sing to El Shaddai with new songs!
Let the faithful assemble to praise Her.
Let all God's people dance for joy before their Creator.
Let Her daughters and sons rejoice in Her presence.
Let them praise Her with dancing and musical instruments.

Surely El Shaddai takes pleasure in Her people.
Surely She adorns Her beloved with peace!

Therefore let the faithful exalt in Her glory.
Let them cry out for joy from their beds.
Let their mouths be filled with the high praises of God.

God's Word accomplishes Her will in this world.
It chastises the peoples and the nations;
it binds all rulers with the demands of obedience.
God requires justice from all those in power,
and threatens unjust leaders with vengeance.
This delights all the faithful!
Alleluia!

Silence

Prayer of the Faithful:

We pray to You, O God, who are the supreme Truth,
    and all truth is from You.
We beseech You, O God, who are the highest Wisdom,
and all the wise depend on You for their wisdom.
You are the supreme Joy, and all who are joyful owe it to You.
You are the greatest Good, and all goodness comes from You.
You are the Light of minds, and all receive their understanding from You.

We love You — indeed, we love You above all things.
We seek You, follow You, and are prepared to serve You.

Alfred the Great, King of England, 849-899

Benediction: May the blessing of God the Creator fill our lives with new possibilities and the joy of creating our own small contribution to the New Creation that is coming. Amen.

EVENING PRAYER

Opening:

I will go to my rest in peace,
for You alone, O God, make me dwell in safety.

Hymn Prayer:

O worship our God, all glorious above;
O gratefully sing Her power and Her love;
our shield and defender, the Ancient of Days,
pavilioned in splendor, and girded with praise.

O tell of Her might, O sing of Her grace,
whose robe is the light, whose canopy space.
Her chariots of fire the deep thunderclouds form,
and dark is Her path on the wings of the storm.

Thy bountiful care what tongue can recite?
It breathes in the air; it shines in the light.
It streams from the hills, it descends to the plain,
and sweetly distills in the dew and the rain.

Frail children of dust, and feeble as frail,
in Thee do we trust, nor find Thee to fail.
Thy mercies how tender, how firm to the end,
our Maker, Defender, Redeemer, and Friend!

Robert Grant, 1833
(text modified by author)

Psalm 135:1-14, 19-21
(This might be the prayer of a Jewish women's group.)

Alleluia!
Praise El Shaddai for who She is!
All You who love and serve Her, come into Her holy presence!
Adore Her as you stand before Her.
Thank Her for all Her goodness!
Offer Her your songs of thanksgiving with delight!
For El Shaddai has chosen us for Herself,
has made us Her own special treasure!

El Shaddai is greater than all other powers.
She does as She pleases in heaven, on earth, and in the depths.
She sets the banks of clouds in the sky,
sends the lightning with the rain,
and unleashes the wind from Her storehouse.

It was She who delivered Her people from Egypt.
With signs and wonders She defeated Pharaoh and all his hosts.
Her name endures forever, the memory of Her through all generations.
She judges all people with justice and shows mercy to all who serve Her.

O house of Sarah, bless El Shaddai!
O house of Miriam, bless El Shaddai!
O house of Deborah, bless El Shaddai!
All Her faithful daughters and sons — bless El Shaddai!
Blessed be She among all Her people,
She who loves to dwell in their midst!
Alleluia!

Reading: Revelation 12:1-6 and 13-17 or selection from the Appendix

Prayer: Intercession for human creativity, the arts, all artists, and the flourishing of beauty in every part of society

Benediction: May God the Word who spoke creation into being; God the Spirit who brooded, and still broods, over the waters of the deep; and God the Artist who shaped us in Her image — may She grant us the power to treasure and tend this beautiful garden of creation. Amen.

Appendix of Readings
for Psalm Prayer

This appendix is made up of selections from the writings of four remarkable women in religious history:

Hildegard of Bingen (1098-1179), theologian, abbess, physician, poet, musician, scientist (and artist)

Mechthild of Magdeburg (1210-1280), writer, reformer of the church, servant of the poor, mystic, and prophet

Julian of Norwich (1342–c. 1419), writer, anchoress, visionary theologian

Theresa of Ávila (1515-1582), theologian, writer, mystic, and religious leader; later one of the few women officially named as a "doctor" of the church.

For the titles of collections of their works, see the Bibliography.

Week One: Sunday

Who is the Holy Spirit?
The Holy Spirit is a Burning Spirit, Who kindles the hearts of humankind,
playing them like tympanum and lyre,
gathering volume in the temple of the soul.

The Holy Spirit is Life-giving-life, all movement, root of all being,
purifier of all impurity, absolver of all faults, balm of all wounds,
radiant life, worthy of all praise.
The Holy Spirit resurrects and awakens everything that is.

Be not lax in celebrating!
Be not lazy in the festive service of God!
Be ablaze with enthusiasm.
Let us be an alive, burning offering before the altar of God!

Hildegard of Bingen

Week One: Monday

The soul is kissed by God in its innermost regions.
With interior yearning, grace and blessing are bestowed.
It is a yearning to take on God's gentle yoke,
It is a yearning to give one's self to God's Way.

The marvels of God are not brought forth from one's self.
Rather, it is more like a chord, a sound that is played.
The tone does not come out of the chord itself, but rather,
through the touch of the Musician.
I am, of course, the lyre and harp of God's kindness!

Hildegard of Bingen

You speak to me of my beginnings?
I will tell you.
I was created in Love.
For that reason, nothing can express my beauty,
nor liberate my nobleness,
except Love alone.

From the very beginning, God loved us.
The Holy Trinity gave itself in the creation of all things,
and made us, body and soul, in infinite love.
We were fashioned most nobly.
God takes such delight in the human person
that Divinity sings this song to our soul:

O love rose on the thorn!
O hovering bee in the honey!
O pure dove in your being!
O glorious sun in your setting!
O full moon in your course!
From you, I your God, will never turn away.

Mechthild of Magdeburg

Week One: Tuesday

Without the Word of God
No creature has being.
God's WORD is in all creation, visible and invisible.
The WORD is living, being, spirit, all verdant greening, all creativity.
All creation is awakened, called, by the resounding melody,
God's invocation of the WORD.

This WORD is manifest in every creature.
Now this is how the spirit is in the flesh —
the WORD is indivisible from GOD.

The more one knows about that which one knows nothing of,
the more one gains in wisdom.
One has, therefore, through science,
eyes with which it behooves us to pay attention.

Who are the prophets?
They are a royal people, who penetrate mystery
and see with the spirit's eyes.
In illuminating darkness they speak out.
They are living, penetrating clarity.
They are a blossom blooming only on the shoot
that is rooted in the flood of light.

Hildegard of Bingen

Week One: Wednesday

Creation is to serve humankind in its bodily needs,
and to be for the health of the soul as well.

The air, with its penetrating strength,
characterizes the victorious banner that is trust.
It gives light to the fire's flame,
and sprinkles the imagination of believers with the dew of hope.

Thus does trust show the way.
Those who breathe this dew long for heavenly things.
They carry within refreshing, fulfilling, greening love,
with which they hasten to the aid of all.
With the passion of heavenly yearning,
they produce rich fruit.

Just like the fishes that dance in the waters of trust,
God feeds the contrite with nourishment of life.

Hildegard of Bingen

Week One: Thursday

Under Your protection, I rejoice, O God!
In Your shadow, I exult, O God!
You rescue me from the heaviness of sin.
My soul anticipates drawing ever closer to You
in the doing of good works.
This supreme longing pulls me to You,
beckons me come under Your protection,
into the shadow of Your power.
I am secure from all enemies there!

The first seed of the longing for Justice
blows through the soul like the wind.
The taste for good will play in it like a breeze.

The consummation of this seed is a greening in the soul
that is like that of the ripening world.
Now the soul honors God by the doing of just deeds.
The soul is only as strong as its work.

Hildegard of Bingen

Week One: Friday

In the aimless, spinning soul where fog obscures the intellect and will,
where the fruit is noxious and poisonous, You guide the pruning knife.
Thus the spirit orders all desire.
But should the soul incline to be covetous and incorrigible,
fixing its gaze on evil's face, looking ever with eyes of malice,
You rush in with fire, and burn, as You will.

O Holy Spirit, Fiery Comforter Spirit, Life of the life of all creatures,
Holy are You, You that give existence to all form.
Holy are You, You that are balm for the mortally wounded.
Holy are You, You that cleanse deep hurt.
Fire of love, Breath of all holiness,
You are so delicious to our hearts.
You infuse our hearts deeply with the good smell of virtue.

Hildegard of Bingen

Week One: Saturday

It is easier to gaze into the Sun than into the face of the mystery of God.
Such is its beauty and its radiance.
God says:
I am the supreme fire; not deadly, but rather,
enkindling every spark of life.

I am the reflection of providence for all.
I am the resounding WORD; the It-Shall-Be
that I intone with mighty power
from which all the world proceeds.
Through animate eyes I divide the seasons of time.
I am aware of what they are.
I am aware of their potential.
With my mouth I kiss my own chosen creation.
I uniquely, lovingly embrace every image
I have made out of the earth's clay.
With a fiery spirit I transform it into a body to serve all the world.

Hildegard of Bingen

Week Two: Sunday

When God was knitted to our body in the Virgin's womb,
God took our Sensuality and oned it to our Substance.
Thus our Lady is our Mother in whom we are all enclosed
and in Christ we are born of her.
And Jesus is our true Mother in whom we are endlessly carried
and out of whom we will never come.

We were all created at the same time;
and in our creation we were knit and oned to God.
By this we are kept as luminous and noble as when we were created.
By the force of this precious oneing we love, seek, praise, thank,
and endlessly enjoy our Creator.

In Jesus we have the skillful and wise keeping of our Sensuality
as well as our restoring and liberation;
for He is our Mother, Brother, and Liberator.

Our whole life is in three —
we have our Being, then our Increasing, and finally our Fulfilling.
The first is Nature, the second Compassion, and the third Grace.

God said:
"This I am — the capability and goodness of the Fatherhood.
This I am — the wisdom of the Motherhood.
This I am — the light and the grace that is all love.
This I am — the Trinity.
This I am — the Unity.
I am the sovereign goodness of all things.
I am what makes you love.
I am what makes you long and desire.
This I am — the endless fulfilling of all desires."

Just as God is truly our Father; just so is God also truly our Mother.
A mother's service is nearest, readiest, and surest.
This office no one person has the ability
or knows how to or ever will do fully but God alone.

Julian of Norwich

Week Two: Monday

I understood that our sensuality is grounded in Nature,
in Compassion, and in Grace.
This enables us to receive gifts that lead to everlasting life.
For I saw that in our sensuality God is.
For God is never out of the soul.
Our soul is trinitarian, like to the uncreated Trinity.
It is known and loved from without beginning,
and in its creation oned to the Creator.

Because of the beautiful oneing that was made by God
between the body and the soul,
it must be that we will be restored from double death.

In the same point that our soul is made sensual,
in the same point is the City of God established from without beginning.
God comes into this seat and never will remove it.
For God is never out of the soul.
God is nearer to us than our own soul,
because God is the ground in which our soul stands
and God is the means whereby our Substance and our Sensuality
are kept together so as to never be apart.

Until our soul is in its full powers, we cannot at all be whole.
By this I mean, when our Sensuality is connected to our Substance
we are made whole through the strength of Christ's suffering
and the benefits of our own.
This is accomplished through compassion and grace.
Both our Substance and Sensuality together
may rightly be called our Soul.
That is because they are both oned in God.
Our Sensuality is the beautiful City in which our Lord Jesus sits
and in which He is enclosed.
Our Substance — of the same nature as Jesus' —
is also enclosed in Him, with the blessed soul of Christ
sitting restfully in the Godhead.

Julian of Norwich

Week Two: Tuesday

"That which is impossible for you is not impossible to me:
I will preserve my word in all things and I will make all things well."

This is the Great Deed that Our God will do.

Our faith is grounded in God's Word and we must let this trust be.
How it will be done we will not know until it is done,
because God wants us to be at ease and at peace,
not troubled or kept from enjoying God.

The fullness of joy is to behold God in everything.
God is the ground, the substance,
the teaching, the teacher,
the purpose, and the reward for which every soul labors.

My own sin will not hinder the working of God's goodness.
As long as we are in this life and find ourselves
foolishly dwelling on sinfulness,
our God tenderly touches us and joyfully calls us, saying:
"Let all your love be, my child.
Turn to Me. I am everything You need.
Enjoy Me and your liberation!"

True thanking is to enjoy God.
Thanking is a true understanding of who we really are.
With reverence and awe we turn ourselves around
towards the working that our good God incites us to do,
enjoying and thanking with our real selves.

God does not want us to be burdened because of sorrows
and tempests that happen in our lives,
because it has always been so before miracles happen.

Julian of Norwich

Week Two: Wednesday

God showed me in my palm a little thing round as a ball
about the size of a hazelnut.
I looked at it with the eye of my understanding and asked myself,
"What is this thing?"

And I was answered: "It is everything that is created."

I wondered how it could survive since it seemed so little
it could suddenly disintegrate into nothing.
The answer came: "It endures and ever will endure, because God loves it."

And so everything has being because of God's love.

Until I am really truly oned and fastened to God
so that there is nothing created between us,
I will never have full rest or complete happiness.
For in order to love and have God who is uncreated,
we must have knowledge of the smallness of creatures
and empty ourselves of all that is created.
We seek rest where there is no rest, and therefore are uneasy.
God is the True Rest who wants to be known.
God finds pleasure in being our true resting place.

God is everything that is good, and the goodness
that everything possesses
is God.
God wants us to allow ourselves to see God continually.
For God wants to be seen and wants to be sought.
God wants to be awaited and wants to be trusted.

Julian of Norwich

Week Two: Thursday

There comes a time when both body and soul
enter into such a vast darkness
that one loses light and consciousness
and knows nothing more of God's intimacy.

At such a time, when the light in the lantern burns out
the beauty of the lantern can no longer be seen,
with longing and distress we are reminded of our nothingness.

At such a time I pray to God:
"O God, this burden is too heavy for me!"
And God replies:
"I will take this burden first and clasp it close to Myself
and that way you may more easily bear it."
But still I feel that I can bear no longer the wounds God has given me,
unanointed and unbound.
My enemies surround me.
O God, how long must I remain here on earth in this mortal body
as a target at which people throw stones and shoot
and assail my honor with their evil cunning?

I am hunted, captured, and bound,
wounded so terribly that I can never be healed.
God has wounded me close unto death.
If God leaves me unanointed, I could never recover.
Even if all the hills flowed with healing oils,
and all the waters contained healing powers,
and all the flowers and all the trees dripped with healing ointments,
still, I could never recover.
God, I will tear the heart of my soul in two
and you must lie therein.
You must lay yourself in the wounds of my soul.

Mechthild of Magdeburg

Week Two: Friday

Humankind does well to keep honesty, to keep to truth.
Those that love lies bring suffering
not only to themselves but to others as well,
since they are driven to ever more lies.
These lies are like juiceless foam, hard and black.
Lacking the verdancy of justice, it is dry,
totally without tender goodness, totally without illuminating virtue.

Now in the people that were meant to green,
there is no more life of any kind.
There is only shriveled barrenness.
The winds are burdened by the utterly awful stink of evil,
selfish goings on.
Thunderstorms menace.
The air belches out the filthy uncleanliness of the peoples.
There pours forth an unnatural, a loathsome darkness,
that withers the green and wizens the fruit
that was to serve as food for the people.
Sometimes this layer of air is full,
full of a fog that is the source of many destructive and barren creatures
that destroy and damage the earth,
rendering it incapable of sustaining humanity.

God desires that all the world be pure in God's sight.
The earth should not be injured.
The earth should not be destroyed.
As often as the elements of the world are violated by ill-treatment,
so God will cleanse them.
God will cleanse them through the sufferings,
through the hardships of humankind.
The high, the low, all of creation,
God gives to humankind to use.
If this privilege is misused,
God's Justice permits creation to punish humanity.

Hildegard of Bingen

Week Two: Saturday

Now it came to pass that man lacked a help-mate that was his equal.
God created this help-mate in the form of a woman,
a mirror image of all that was latent in the male sex.
In this way, man and woman are so intimately related
that one is the work of the other.
Man cannot be called man without woman.
Neither can woman be named woman without man.

Thus, humankind, man and woman, is enthroned over creation
and all creatures are in the care of men and women.
Humankind, in this way, is more than creation.
It is the guardian of creation.

In Nature, God established humankind in power.
We are dressed in the scaffold of creation:
in seeing — to recognize all the world,
in hearing — to understand,
in smelling — to discern,
in tasting — to nurture,
in touching — to govern.
In this way humankind comes to know God,
for God is the author of all creation.
Now God has built the human form into the world structure,
indeed even the cosmos,
just as an artist would use a particular pattern in her work.
And so, humankind, full of all creative possibilities,
is God's work.
Humankind alone is called to assist God.
Humankind is called to co-create.

Hildegard of Bingen

Week Three: Sunday

Woman, you must adorn yourself!
Maiden, you ought to dance merrily, dance like my elected one!
Dance like the noblest, loveliest, richest queen!

And, if you meet Me with the flowering desire of flowing love,
then must I touch you with my Divine nature as my queen.

Then you shall soar forever and delight — soul and body —
in my Holy Trinity, immersed like a fish in the sea.
For the fish cannot live long stranded on the shore.

"I cannot dance, O God, unless You lead me.
If You will that I leap joyfully, then You must be the first to dance
    and to sing!
Then, and only then, will I leap for love.
Then will I soar from love to knowledge,
from knowledge to fruition,
from fruition to beyond all human sense.
And there I will remain and circle forevermore."

I once heard the Spirit speak to the Creator, saying:
"We will no longer be unfruitful! We will have a creative kingdom."
And then I heard Jesus speak to the Creator, saying:
"My nature too must bear fruit.
Together we shall work wonders.
So, let us fashion human beings after the Pattern of myself."

The Holy Spirit flows through us with the marvelous Creative Power
of everlasting joy!

As love grows and expands in the soul, it rises eagerly to God
and overflows towards the Glory which bends towards it.
Then Love melts through the soul into the senses,
so that the body too might share in it,
for Love is drawn into all things.

Mechthild of Magdeburg

Week Three: Monday

If you should at times fall, don't become discouraged
    and stop striving to advance.
For even from this fall, God will draw out good.
Even though we may not find someone to teach us,
    God will guide everything for our benefit,
provided that we don't give up.
There is no other remedy for this evil of giving up prayer
    than to begin again.
Otherwise, the soul will gradually lose more each day,
and, please God, it will understand this fact.

The door of entry to the interior castle (of the soul) is prayer.

Now it is foolish to think that we will enter heaven
    without entering into ourselves,
coming to know our weakness,
and what we owe God, while begging for the mercy of God.

There is no remedy in the tempest of darkness and confusion
but to wait for the mercy of God.
For at an unexpected time, with one word alone, or a chance happening,
God so quickly calms the soul that it seems that there had not been
even as much as a cloud in that soul,
and it remains filled with sunlight and much more consolation.

In the state of darkness, grace is so hidden that
    not even a tiny spark is visible.
These experiences are indescribable, for they are
    spiritual afflictions and sufferings
and one does not know what to call them.

It should not be thought that the faculties, senses,
    and passions are always in peace!
The soul is, yes. But in those other dwelling places,
times of struggle, trial, and fatigue are never lacking.
However, they are such that they do not as a rule
    take the soul from its place of peace.

That there are trials and sufferings
and that at the same time the soul is at peace is difficult to explain.
In this temple of God, in this, God's dwelling place within,
God alone and the soul rejoice together in the deepest quiet.
Perhaps the reason is that God has now fortified, enlarged, and made
    the soul capable.

Teresa of Ávila

Week Three: Tuesday

We are incomparably stupid when we do not strive to know who we are,
but limit ourselves to considering only roughly these bodies.

We have heard and, because faith tells us that we have souls, we know.
But seldom do we consider the precious things that can be found in this soul
or Who dwells in it or its high value.
Consequently, little effort is made to preserve its beauty.

All our attention is taken up with the plainness of the diamond's setting
or the outer walls of the castle; that is, with these bodies of ours.
We must consider our very souls to be like a castle made out of a diamond
or of very clear-cut crystal in which there are many dwellings.
The soul of the just person is nothing else but a paradise where God
    finds delight.

It is like a castle with many dwelling places; some up above,
    others down below, others to the side.
In the center and middle are the dwelling places where
    the very sweet exchanges
of love between God and the soul take place.

The door of entry to this castle is prayer and reflection.

O God, take into account the things we suffer on our path
        for lack of knowledge!
The trouble is that since we do not think there is anything to know
other than what we must think of You,
we do not even know how to ask those whom we know,
nor do we understand what there is to ask!
We suffer terrible trials because we don't understand ourselves,
and that which isn't bad at all, but good, we think is a serious fault.

                                                    Teresa of Ávila

Week Three: Wednesday

It is proper to the royal rule of God to have a privy council
        free from disturbance!
And it is proper that those who serve God do not pry into this council
out of obedience and reverence.
God understands and has compassion on those of us who make
        ourselves so busy trying
to pry into what is none of our business.
I am sure that if we knew how pleasing it would be to God,
not to mention how much easier it would be on ourselves,
we would let go of this nosiness!
Even the saints in heaven have no desire to know what God
        does not want them to know.
We ought to be like them, since we are all one in God's sight.
We must trust, and be glad for everything.

Often our trust is not full.
We are not certain that God hears us, because we
        consider ourselves worthless and as nothing.
This is ridiculous and the cause of our weakness.
I have felt this way myself!

"That which is impossible for you is not impossible to Me:
I will preserve My Word in all things, and I will make all things well."

This is the Great Deed our God will do.

Our faith is grounded in God's Word and we must let this faith be.
How it will be done we will not know until it is done,
because God wants us to be at ease and at peace, not troubled
    or kept from enjoying God.

Faith is nothing else but a right understanding of our being —
trusting and allowing things to be —
a right understanding that we are in God
and God, Whom we do not see, is in us!

In spite of all our feelings of sorrow or well-being
God wants us to understand and know by faith
that we are more truly in heaven than on earth!

Julian of Norwich

Week Three: Thursday

I had a desire to see Hell and Purgatory —
not to have proof that they exist, but rather to learn everything
I had been taught in my faith, so that my life might profit
    from this experience.

But for all my desire I did not see them.
I understood this to mean that God and all the holy ones
no more talk about them than they do about the devil.

The more we busy ourselves to know God's secrets,
the further away from knowledge we shall be.

God wants to be known and loved through Justice and Compassion,
    now and forever.
Justice is that thing that is so good that it cannot be better than it is.
For God is Justice.
God creates Justice in all who will be liberated through goodness.

My own sin need not hinder the working of God's goodness.
As long as we are in this life, and find ourselves foolishly
    dwelling on sinfulness,
our God tenderly touches us and joyfully calls us, saying:
"Let all your love be, my child.
Turn to Me. I am everything you need.
Enjoy Me and your liberation."

Julian of Norwich

When a person understands Justice, the self is let go.
The just taste and drink virtue.
This strengthens them, as if they were addicted to wine,
yet they are never beside themselves, are never uncontrollable,
or know not what they do, as is the case with drunkards.

The just love God, of Whom there can be no surfeit,
    only utter, constant ecstasy.

Hildegard of Bingen

Week Three: Friday

I saw a great oneing between Christ and us,
because when He was in pain we were in pain.
All creatures of God's creation that can suffer pain suffered with Him.
The sky and the earth failed at the time of Christ's dying
because He too was part of nature.
Thus, those who were His friends suffered pain, because they loved Him.

God assigns no blame to the grumblings and curses made
    by the flesh in pain
without the consent of the soul.
The soul, that noble and joyful life that is all peace and love,
draws the flesh to give its consent by grace,
and both shall be oned in eternal happiness.

God said: "It is necessary that sin should exist.
But, all will be well, and all will be well, and every manner
    of thing will be well!"

I did not see sin,
for I believe that it has no kind of substance nor any part of being,
nor could it be known except by the pain it causes.
And this pain purges us and makes us know ourselves
and to ask compassion.

God showed two sorts of sickness that we have:
The one is our lack of ability to endure, or sloth — for we bear
    our toils and pains heavily.
The other is despair, or fearful awe. . . .
These two are the sins that cause the most pain and turmoil for us.

It would be contrary to nature to put blame on God
or show any lack of trust because of *my* sin
since God does not blame me.

Just as God courteously forgives our sin after we change our ways,
so also does God want *us* to forgive *our* sin
instead of falling into a false humility that is really a foul
    blindness and weakness
due to fear.

                                         Julian of Norwich

Week Three: Saturday

(God says)
"I, the fiery Life of Divine Wisdom —
I ignite the beauty of the plains,
I sparkle the waters,
I burn in the sun, and the moon, and the stars.
With Wisdom I order All rightly.
Above All I determine truth.

I am the One whose praise echoes on high.
I adorn all the earth.
I am the Breath that nurtures all things green.
I encourage blossoms to flourish with ripening fruits.
I feed the purest streams . . .
I am the rain coming from the dew that causes the grasses
        to laugh with the joy of life.
I call forth tears, the aroma of holy work.
I am the yearning for good."

Holy Spirit, through You clouds billow, breezes blow,
        stones drip with trickling streams,
streams that are the source of earth's lush greening.
Likewise, You are the source of human understanding.

You bless with the Breath of Wisdom.
Thus all of our praise is Yours,
You Who are the melody itself of praise,
the joy of life, the mighty honor, the hope of those
        to whom You give the gifts of the Light.

Limitless Love, from the depths to the stars!
Flooding all, loving all, It is the royal kiss of peace!

                                    Hildegard of Bingen

Week Four: Sunday

Food is shut in within our bodies as in a very beautiful purse.
When necessity calls, the purse opens and then shuts again,
    in the most fitting way.
And it is God Who does this, because I was shown that
    the Goodness of God
permeates us ever even in our most humble needs.
God does not despise any part of creation, nor does God disdain to serve us
in the simplest function that belongs to our bodies in nature,
because God loves us and we are made in the image of God.

                                   Julian of Norwich

Divine Love is so immensely great!
Great is its overflow, for Divine Love is never still.
Always ceaselessly and tirelessly it pours itself out
so that the small vessel which is ourselves might be filled to the brim
and might also overflow.

The rippling tide of Love flows secretly out from God
into the soul, and draws it mightily back to its Source.

Love wanders about through the senses
and then it storms the soul with all its powers.
In the heart of this maid
I saw a spring of Living Water welling up.

From the overflowing love of God there flows evermore into the soul
a sweet, longing, hungry love.

What is this greatest kind of love?
Great love does not flow with tears.
Rather, it burns in the great Fire of Heaven.
In this Fire, it flows and flows swiftly
yet all the while it remains in itself in a very great stillness.

                              Mechthild of Magdeburg

Week Four: Monday

Fidelity sees God and Wisdom keeps God close by,
and from these two comes Love — a delight in God
    completely steeped in wonder.
God created all three.
Our soul, a creature in God, possesses all three and evermore does all three
for this is the purpose of its creation.
We were made for Love.

We will all enter our God, fully aware of and fully possessing God.
This will last forever.
We will truly see, fully feel, spiritually hear, delectably breathe in,
and sweetly drink God.

Our soul must perform two duties.
The one is, we must reverently wonder and be surprised;
the other is, we must gently let go and let be, always taking pleasure in God.
Seeing God in this life cannot be a continuous experience.
We often fail to see God, and then we fall into ourselves
and feel there is something wrong with us —
that we are perverse and responsible for the entrance of sin into the world
and all subsequent sins.
These feelings affect us mentally and physically.
But the Holy Spirit, the endless life living within us,
makes us peaceful and at ease, harmonious and flexible.

I saw wrath and vengeance only on our part.
God forgives that in us.
For wrath is a turning away from peace and love, and is opposed to them.
It comes from a failing of power, or of wisdom, or of goodness on our part.

The ground of Compassion is love, and the working
    of Compassion keeps us in love.
Compassion is a sweet, gracious working in love, mingled
    with abundant kindness:
for Compassion works at taking care of us and
    makes all things become good.
Compassion allows us to fail measurably and inasmuch as we fail,

in so much we fall; and in so much as we fall, in so much we die;
for we must die if we fail to see and feel God, Who is our life.
Our failing is fearful, our falling is shameful, and our dying is sorrowful:
but in all this the sweet eye of kindness and love never leaves us,
nor does the working of Compassion cease.

Compassion is a kind and gentle property that belongs
    to the Motherhood in tender love.
And grace is a beautiful property which belongs
    to the royal Lordship in the same love.
Compassion protects, increases our sensitivity, gives life, and heals.
Grace rebuilds, rewards, endlessly disregarding what we deserve,
spreading widely and showing the greatly abundant and generous hospitality
of the royal Lordship in God's astonishing courtesy towards us.

Julian of Norwich

Week Four: Tuesday

God is everlasting truth.
I am reminded of Pilate, how he was questioning our Lord
    when during the Passion he asked,
"What is truth?"
and of the little we understand about this Supreme Truth.

Let us conclude that in order to live in conformity with our God and spouse,
it will be well if we always study diligently how to walk in this Truth.
Especially, there should be no desire that others consider us
    better than we are.
And in our works we should attribute to God what is God's
and to ourselves what is ours, and strive
    to draw out the Truth in everything.

Once I was pondering why our Lord was so fond of this virtue of humility,
and this thought came to me, not as a result of reflection, but suddenly.
It is because God is supreme Truth; and to be humble is to walk in Truth.
For it is a very deep truth that apart from God we have nothing good
but only emptiness and nothingness.

Whoever does not understand this walks in falsehood.
The more anyone understands it, the more this pleases the supreme Truth
because the person is walking in truth.

Please God, we will be granted the favor never
    to leave this path of self-knowledge.

People will tell you that you do not need friends
    on this journey, that God is enough.

But to be with God's friends is a good way to keep close to God in this life.
You will always draw great benefit from them.

This is to love:
bear with a fault and do not be astonished;
relieve others of their labor and take upon yourselves tasks to be done;
be cheerful when others have need of it;
be grateful for your strength when others have need of it;
show tenderness in love and sympathize with the weakness of others.

Friends of God love others far more, with a truer,
    more ardent, and more helpful love.
They are always prepared to give much more readily than
    to receive — even to their Creator.

Teresa of Ávila

Week Four: Wednesday

The fruit and the purpose of prayer is to be oned with
  and like God in all things.

It is the will of God that our prayer and our trust be large.
We must truly know that our God is the ground
  from which our prayer sprouts
and that it is a gift given out of love.
Otherwise, we waste our time and pain ourselves.

When we think that our prayers have not been answered,
we should not become depressed over it.
I am certain that God is telling us that we must wait for a better time,
more grace, or that a better gift will be given us.

God is being, and wants us to sit, dwell, and ground ourselves
  in this knowledge,
while at the same time realizing that we are noble, excellent,
assessed as precious and valuable, and have been given creation
  for our enjoyment
because we are loved!

Prayer ones the soul to God.
Although we are always like God in nature and substance,
having been made whole by grace,
we are often unlike God in our sinful ways.

Prayer is therefore a witness to the fact that we want what God wants,
and this strengthens our conscience and empowers us with Grace.

We should desire to regard God with wondering reverence, rather than fear,
loving God gently and trusting with all we are capable of.
For when we regard God with awe and love God gently,
our trust is never in vain.
The more we trust, and the more powerful this trust,
the more we please and praise our God whom we trust in.
Without this, we cannot please God.

Julian of Norwich

Alas! No, in my old age I find much to criticize,
    for it can produce no shining works;
it can be cold and without grace.
Life appears powerless now that it no longer has youth
to help it endure the fiery love of God.
It is impatient — little ills afflict it much which in youth
    it noticed hardly at all.
Yes, a good old age must be full of patient waiting, and trusts in God alone.

We are invited by God in the following manner:
"Fly, dove-winged one, and soar in all things beyond yourself.
And when you are tired and weary, return to the ark again."

God is not only fatherly.
God is also mother who lifts Her loved child from the ground to Her knee.
The Trinity is like a mother's cloak wherein the child finds a home
and lays its head on the maternal breast.

                                        Mechthild of Magdeburg

Week Four: Thursday

If you love the justice of Jesus Christ more than you fear human judgment
then you will seek to do compassion.
Compassion means that if I see my friend and my enemy in equal need,
I shall help both equally.
Justice demands that we seek and find the stranger, the broken, the prisoner
and comfort them and offer them our help.

Here lies the holy compassion of God that causes the devils so much distress.

Who is the Holy Spirit?
The Holy Spirit is a compassionate outpouring of the Creator and the Son.
That is why, when we on earth pour out compassion and mercy
from the depths of our hearts
and give to the poor, and dedicate our bodies to the service of the broken,
to that very extent do we resemble the Holy Spirit.

When are we like God? I will tell you.
Insofar as we love compassion and practice it steadfastly,
to that extent do we resemble the heavenly Creator
Who practices these things ceaselessly in us.

The noblest joy of the senses, the holiest peace of the heart,
the most resplendent luster of all good works derives from this:
that the creature puts his or her heart wholly into what s/he does.

                                        Mechthild of Magdeburg

Our spiritual eye is so blind, and we are so borne down
        by the weight of our mortal flesh
and the darkness of sin,
that we are not able to see our God's joyful Face — not at all!
Because of this darkness, allowing and trusting God's great love
        and keeping providence
is almost impossible.

Some of us believe that God is All-Power and can do all,
and that God is All-Wisdom and knows how to do all.
But that God is All-Love, and wants to do all,
here we restrain ourselves.
And this ignorance hinders most of God's lovers, as I see it.

                                        Julian of Norwich

Week Four: Friday

We see so much evil around us, so much harm done,
that we think it impossible that there is any good in this world.
We look at this in sorrow and mourn, so that we cannot see God
     as we should.

This is because we use our reason so blindly, so unfully
     and so simplemindedly
that we are unable to know the marvelous wisdom, capability, and goodness
of the joyful Trinity.

Just as the joyful Trinity created all things out of nothing,
so also this same blessed Trinity will make well all that is not well.

God showed me that we should not feel guilty because of sin,
     for sin is valuable.
Just as truth answers every sin by pain,
so also is happiness given to the soul by Love.
Just as different sins are punished with different pains
     according to their seriousness,
so also will these same sins be rewarded with different joys in heaven
according to the amount of pain and sorrow they have caused
     the soul on earth.

For we are all precious to God, and God would never have us come there
without rewarding us for our failing.

Peace and love are always in us, being and working;
but we are not always in peace and love.
God is ground of our whole life in Love, and wants us to know this.
God is also our everlasting keeper and wants us to know this.
God is our friend Who keeps us tenderly while we are in sin,
and touches us privately, showing us where we went wrong
by the sweet light of compassion and grace,
even though we imagine that we will be punished.

I saw no vengeance in God, not for a short time, nor for a long —
for as I see it, if God were vengeful, even for a brief moment,
we would never have life, place, or being.

In God is endless friendship, space, life, and being.

I knew by the common teaching of Holy Church and by my own feeling
that the blame for our sins clings to us continually while we are on this
    earth.

How amazing it was, then, to see our God showing us no more blame
than if we were as clean and whole as the Angels in heaven!

Julian of Norwich

Week Four: Saturday

With nature's help, humankind can set into creation
all that is necessary and life-sustaining.

God's majesty is glorified in the manifestation of every manner
        of nature's fruitfulness.
This is possible through the right and holy utilization of the earth,
the earth in which humankind has its source.

The sum total of heaven and earth, everything in nature, is thus won
        to use and purpose.
It becomes a temple and altar for the service of God.

(God says)

"I have been moved by the form of humankind.
I have kissed it, grounding it in faithful relationship.
Thus, I have exalted humankind with the vocation of creation.
I call humankind to the same norm."

Humankind demonstrates two aspects: the singing of praise to God,
    and the doing of good works.

God is made known through praise, and in good works,
    the wonders of God can be seen.
In the praise of God a person is like an angel.
But it is the doing of good works that is the hallmark of humanity.
This completeness makes humankind the fullest creation of God.

It is in praise and service that the surprise of God is consummated!

The work of God, God brings to fullness in humankind.

Humankind: fashioned in God's image and in God's likeness,
inscribed in God's every creation,
forever in the plan of God, the completion of God's work.

This work's consummation is the giving to humankind of the entire creation,
that women and men might work it to fullness in the selfsame manner
in which God imaged humankind.

Hildegard of Bingen

A song to Mary:

Mary, the heavens gift the grass with moist dew.
The entire earth rejoices.
From your womb the seed sprouted forth.
The birds of the air nest in this Tree.

Blessed is the fruit of your womb!
Your womb's fruitfulness is Food for humankind.
Great is the joy at this delicious banquet!
In you, mild virgin, is the Fullness of all joy.

You, glowing, most green, verdant sprout,
in the movement of the Spirit,
in the midst of wise and holy seekers,
You bud forth into light.

Your time to blossom has come!
Balsam scented, in you the beautiful Flower blossomed.
It is the beautiful Flower that lends its scent to those herbs,
all that had shriveled and wilted.
It brings them lush greenness once more.

                                        Hildegard of Bingen

Bibliography

Campbell, Camille. *Meditations with Teresa of Avila*. Santa Fe, New Mexico: Bear & Company, 1985.

Doyle, Brendan. *Meditations with Julian of Norwich*. Santa Fe, New Mexico: Bear & Company, 1983.

Fischer, Clare B., et al., eds. *Women in a Strange Land*. Philadelphia: Fortress Press, 1975.

Holy Bible: New Revised Standard Version. Grand Rapids: Zondervan Bible Publishers, 1990.

The Hymnbook. Published by the PCUSA, UPC, and RCA. Richmond, Philadelphia, and New York, 1955.

Mollenkott, Virginia Ramey. *The Divine Feminine*. New York: Crossroad, 1983.

People's Prayer Book. New York: Catholic Book Publishing Co., 1980.

Psalter Hymnal. Grand Rapids: CRC Publications, 1987.

Rae, Eleanor, and Marie-Daly, Bernice. *Created in Her Image*. New York: Crossroad, 1990.

Rejoice in the Lord. Grand Rapids: William B. Eerdmans, 1985.

The Revised Standard Edition of the Bible. New York: Oxford University Press, 1973 and 1977.

Ruether, Rosemary Radford. *Religion and Sexism*. New York: Simon & Schuster, 1974.

Russell, Letty. *Human Liberation in a Feminist Perspective — A Theology*. Philadelphia: Westminster Press, 1974.

Thistlethwaite, Susan Brooks, and Engel, Mary Potter, eds. *Lift Every Voice*. San Francisco: Harper & Row, 1990.

Uhlein, Gabriele. *Meditations with Hildegard of Bingen*. Santa Fe, New Mexico: Bear & Company, 1982.

Ulanov, Ann Belford. *Picturing God*. Cambridge, Mass.: Cowley Publications, 1986.

The United Methodist Hymnal. Nashville: United Methodist Publishing House, 1989.

Von Wartenberg-Potter, Barbel. *We Will Not Hang Our Harps on the Willows*. Oak Park, Ill.: Meyer-Stone Books, 1988.

Woodruff, Sue. *Meditations with Mechtild of Magdeburg*. Sante Fe, New Mexico: Bear & Company, 1982.

Wren, Brian. *What Language Shall I Borrow?* New York: Crossroad, 1990.

Liturgical Index

These Psalms can be read in such a way that they correspond to the liturgical seasons.

For the Advent season, the Psalms for Monday are suggested (pp. 11-17, 63-69, 120-26, 177-84).

For the Epiphany season, the Psalms for Wednesday are suggested (pp. 18-24, 70-76, 127-34, 185-90).

For the Lenten season, the Psalms for Thursday and Friday are suggested (pp. 32-38, 84-92, 142-50, 199-206; and pp. 39-45, 93-102, 151-56, 207-14).

For the Easter season, the Psalms for Sunday are suggested (pp. 3-10, 55-62, 113-19, 167-76).

For Pentecost and Ordinary Time extending through the summer, the Psalms for Tuesday are suggested (pp. 25-31, 77-83, 135-41, 191-98).

For Ordinary Time extending from Fall until Advent, the Psalms for Saturday are suggested (pp. 46-52, 103-9, 157-64, 215-20).

Psalm Index

Psalm	Page		Psalm	Page		Psalm	Page
Psalm 1	18		Psalm 36	81		Psalm 73	182
Psalm 2	13		Psalm 37	21		Psalm 74	158
Psalm 3	30		Psalm 38	97		Psalm 75	180
Psalm 4	30		Psalm 39	98		Psalm 76	14
Psalm 5	4		Psalm 40	121		Psalm 77	155
Psalm 6	44		Psalm 41	143		Psalm 78	169
Psalm 7	34		Psalm 42	208		Psalm 81	179
Psalm 8	51		Psalm 43	56		Psalm 82	149
Psalm 10	87		Psalm 46	178		Psalm 84	9
Psalm 11	28		Psalm 47	114		Psalm 85	16
Psalm 12	33		Psalm 48	114		Psalm 86	144
Psalm 13	28		Psalm 49	19		Psalm 87	115
Psalm 14	42		Psalm 50	118		Psalm 88	209
Psalm 15	4		Psalm 51	153		Psalm 89	216
Psalm 16	10		Psalm 52	79		Psalm 90	193
Psalm 17	37		Psalm 54	33		Psalm 91	197
Psalm 18	66, 68		Psalm 55	145		Psalm 92	23
Psalm 19	71		Psalm 56	148		Psalm 93	107
Psalm 20	123		Psalm 57	12		Psalm 94	140
Psalm 22	40		Psalm 58	200		Psalm 95	105
Psalm 23	26		Psalm 59	200		Psalm 96	105
Psalm 24	56		Psalm 61	44		Psalm 97	122
Psalm 25	94		Psalm 62	192		Psalm 98	180
Psalm 26	58		Psalm 63	125		Psalm 99	58
Psalm 27	61		Psalm 64	202		Psalm 100	116
Psalm 28	78		Psalm 65	104		Psalm 101	24
Psalm 29	47		Psalm 66	168		Psalm 102	95
Psalm 30	115		Psalm 67	48		Psalm 103	26
Psalm 31	85		Psalm 68	170		Psalm 104	158
Psalm 32	151		Psalm 69	210		Psalm 107	161
Psalm 33	64		Psalm 70	204		Psalm 108	65
Psalm 34	136		Psalm 71	204		Psalm 111	72
Psalm 35	90		Psalm 72	174		Psalm 112	137